First World War
and Army of Occupation
War Diary
France, Belgium and Germany

50 DIVISION
151 Infantry Brigade
Border Regiment
5th Battalion
27 December 1915 - 31 January 1918

WO95/2843/4

The Naval & Military Press Ltd
www.nmarchive.com
Published in association with The National Archives

Published by

The Naval & Military Press Ltd

Unit 10 Ridgewood Industrial Park,

Uckfield, East Sussex,

TN22 5QE England

Tel: +44 (0) 1825 749494

www.naval-military-press.com

www.nmarchive.com

This diary has been reprinted in facsimile from the original. Any imperfections are inevitably reproduced and the quality may fall short of modern type and cartographic standards.

© **Crown Copyright**
Images reproduced by permission of The National Archives, London, England, 2015.

Contents

Document type	Place/Title	Date From	Date To
Heading	WO95/2843/4 5 Bn Border Regt. 1915 Del-1918 Jan		
Heading	50th Division 151st Infy Bde 1-5th Bn Border Regt Dec 1915-Jan 1918 From 149 Bde 50 Div To 32 Div 97 Bde		
War Diary		27/12/1915	18/02/1916
Heading	1/5 Border Regt Vol VI 151 Bde		
War Diary		22/02/1916	02/03/1916
Miscellaneous	D.A.G. 3rd Echelon.	28/04/1916	28/04/1916
War Diary		06/03/1916	31/03/1916
Miscellaneous	To O.C. 5th Bn The Border Regiment. Appendix F	06/03/1916	06/03/1916
Miscellaneous			
Miscellaneous	D.A.G. Base.	15/05/1916	15/05/1916
War Diary		02/04/1916	30/04/1916
Miscellaneous	5th Battalion The Border Regiment. Particulars Of Officers.		
War Diary		23/05/1916	29/06/1916
Miscellaneous	D.A.G. 3rd Echelon, G.H.Q. Base.	30/06/1916	30/06/1916
Miscellaneous	5th Battalion The Border Regiment. Particulars Of Officers.		
Heading	5th Bn. The Border Regt. War Diary. July 1916. Volume No. 2		
War Diary		30/06/1916	01/07/1916
War Diary	M&N. Trenches	01/07/1916	09/07/1916
War Diary	La Clytte	10/07/1916	16/07/1916
War Diary	D&E Trenches.	19/07/1916	23/07/1916
War Diary	Locre	24/07/1916	25/07/1916
War Diary	Trenches. E1., E.2, F.2. F.4., F.5, And Supports.	26/07/1916	31/07/1916
Miscellaneous	151st Infantry Brigade.	27/07/1916	27/07/1916
Heading	War Diary 1/5th Battn The Border Regt. August 1916 Volume No. 9.		
War Diary		01/08/1916	01/08/1916
War Diary	Aircraft Farm. Kemmel	01/08/1916	06/08/1916
War Diary	Boeschepe.	06/08/1916	10/08/1916
War Diary	Divisional Move.	11/08/1916	11/08/1916
War Diary	Godewaersvelde	11/08/1916	11/08/1916
War Diary	Vignacourt	15/08/1916	16/08/1916
War Diary	Rainneville	16/08/1916	16/08/1916
War Diary	Baizieux Wood	17/08/1916	31/08/1916
Heading	151st. Infantry Brigade 50th. Division 5th. Border Regt. 151st Infantry Brigade September 1916.		
Heading	5 Bn. The Border Regt September, 1916. Volume No. 12		
War Diary	Baizieux Wood.	01/09/1916	16/09/1916
War Diary		15/09/1916	30/09/1916
Miscellaneous	151st Infantry Brigade.	01/11/1916	01/11/1916
War Diary		01/10/1916	31/10/1916
War Diary	5th Battalion The Border Regiment Particulars Of Officers.		
Heading	War Diary. 5th Border Regt. November, 1916 Volume 14		

War Diary		01/11/1916	30/11/1916
Heading	War Diary 5th Bn. The Border Regt. 30th November to 31st December Volume No. 13		
War Diary		01/12/1916	31/12/1916
War Diary	War Diary. 5th Bn. The Border Regiment. January, 1917. Volume No. 13.		
War Diary		04/01/1917	31/01/1917
Heading	War Diary. 5th Bn. The Border Regt. February 1917. Volume 14.		
War Diary	Ribemont.	01/02/1917	10/02/1917
War Diary	Morcourt.	11/02/1917	12/02/1917
War Diary	Bois. St Martin.	12/02/1917	18/02/1917
War Diary	Faucaucourt	19/02/1917	28/02/1917
Heading	5th Bn. The Border Regt. March, 1917. Volume 15.		
War Diary		01/03/1917	27/03/1917
War Diary		16/03/1917	31/03/1917
Heading	War Diary 5th Bn The Border Regt. Volume 16 For April, 1917.		
War Diary	Talmas	01/04/1917	02/04/1917
War Diary	Gezaincourt	03/04/1917	03/04/1917
War Diary	G. Bouriet	04/04/1917	04/04/1917
War Diary	Siracourt	05/04/1917	07/04/1917
War Diary	Ternas	08/04/1917	10/04/1917
War Diary	Gouves	11/04/1917	11/04/1917
War Diary	Ronville	12/04/1917	15/04/1917
War Diary	The Caves Arras	16/04/1917	30/04/1917
Heading	War Diary 5th Bn The Border Regt. Volume 17 May, 1917		
War Diary		01/05/1917	31/05/1917
Heading	War Diary 5th Bn. The Border Regiment, T.F. June, 1917. Volume 18.		
War Diary		01/06/1917	30/06/1917
Heading	War Diary 5th Bn The Border Regt July 1917 Volume No XIX		
Heading	Tape Party		
Operation(al) Order(s)	Operation Orders By Major J.L. Henderson DSO Comd 5th Bn The Border Regt		
War Diary Miscellaneous		01/07/1917	31/07/1917
Heading	War Diary 5th Bn. Border Regiment. August, 1917. Volume-XX		
War Diary Miscellaneous		01/08/1917	31/08/1917
Heading	War Diary 5th Border Regiment September, 1917. Volume-XXI.		
War Diary		01/09/1917	29/09/1917
War Diary Miscellaneous		26/09/1917	30/09/1917
Heading	War Diary 5th Border Regiment. October, 1917. Volume XXII		
War Diary		01/10/1917	30/10/1917
War Diary		16/10/1917	31/10/1917
Heading	War Diary 5th Bn. The Border Regiment November, 1917 Volume-XXXII		
War Diary		01/11/1917	30/11/1917
War Diary		31/10/1917	06/11/1917

Heading	War Diary 5th Bn. The Border Regiment December, 1917 Volume No XXIV		
War Diary		01/12/1917	31/12/1917
Heading	War Diary 5th Bn. The Border Regiment January, 1918 Volume-XXV.		
War Diary		01/01/1918	31/01/1918

WO 95 2843/4

5 BN BORDER REGT.
1915 DEC — 1918 JAN

50TH DIVISION
151ST INFY BDE

1-5TH BN BORDER REGT
DEC 1915-JAN 1918

FROM 149 BDE 50 DIV

TO 32 DN 97 BDE ✓ OK

Army Form C. 2118.

WAR DIARY
or
INTELLIGENCE SUMMARY.
(Erase heading not required.)

Instructions regarding War Diaries and Intelligence
Summaries are contained in F.S. Regs., Part II.
and the Staff Manual respectively. Title pages
will be prepared in manuscript.

Hour, Date, Place	Summary of Events and Information	Remarks and references to Appendices
27th December 1915.	During the period in reserve the Battalion supplied fatigue and working parties for R.E. &c. and kept communication trenches to in repair.	
31st December 1915.	Battalion took over trenches in front line.	
1st January 1916.	During the night 31st December/1st January our artillery fired on the enemy trenches. He did not retaliate. The Germans sang and shouted throughout the night and a band in their lines played "God save the King". During Christmas and the New Year no truce was observed. Following message received from the Earl of Lonsdale:- "That New Year brings you all you desire with victorious peace is my sincerest wish – Lonsdale". Seasonable greetings were also received from 2/5th, 3/5th and Administrative Centre.	
2nd January 1916.	Nothing of interest to report. The enemy continues persistent sniping.	
3rd January 1916.	Past 24 hours generally quiet. At 5.30 a.m. 3rd enemy sent up a red flare on the right. This was followed by a considerable amount of artillery fire on both sides. At 6-10a.m. the enemy sent up another red flare, but nothing unusual followed. Our artillery shelled an enemy transport which retired at full speed leaving casualties behind. Sniping and rifle fire on the part of the enemy was much less than last night. At 5.30p.m. the enemy sent up a red flare, but nothing unusual followed.	
4th January 1916.	Battalion relieved in trenches and proceeded to DICKEBUSCH Huts.	

WAR DIARY
or
INTELLIGENCE SUMMARY.
(Erase heading not required.)

Army Form C. 2118.

Hour, Date, Place	Summary of Events and Information	Remarks and references to Appendices
4th to 8th January 1916.	Battalion in Divisional Reserve in DICKEBUSCH Huts.	
9th January 1916.	Battalion relieved 6th Bn D.L.I. in trenches A7 to A12.	
10th January 1916.	Night quiet and rifle fire practically nil. Between 3-45am and 4-45am, 10th Jany. Heavy gun and rifle fire heard on the right.	
11th January 1916.	Enemy shelled area on the right for about 1 hour commencing 2-30pm. 10th inst. Area shelled included trenches A.7. A.8 and A.9 and their communication trenches. Our artillery replied but the enemy did not cease shelling. Battalion casualties were 6 killed and 4 wounded.	
12th January 1916.	An enemy digging party was observed yesterday and was scattered by our artillery. One of them was seen distinctly to be wearing closely fitting blue clothes and a civilian cap. A cloud of white smoke rose from the enemy's line at 7.30am today and flew back over their trenches. They may have been testing the wind. Three pigeons flew from the enemy's lines opposite trench A11 this morning. They were followed by two more. All flew in the direction of MAPLE COPSE.	
13th January 1916.	Officers patrol from trench A11 at 5-30 am went up an old French trench to the German lines and proceeded along it for a distance of some sixty yards. It afforded good cover for some way up but afterwards became decker and very wet. In a small trench behind quite a good dugout was found and some British S.A.A.	
13th January 1916.	Battalion relieved in front line by 6th D.L.I. and went back into Brigade Reserve with Companies distributed as follows:— "A" Company - SANCTUARY WOOD DUGOUTS. "B" " - CANAL BANKS "C" " - REDOUBTS. "D" " - MAPLE COPSE. Grenadiers - MAPLE COPSE.	

Army Form C. 2118.

WAR DIARY
or
INTELLIGENCE SUMMARY.
(Erase heading not required.)

Instructions regarding War Diaries and Intelligence Summaries are contained in F. S. Regs., Part II. and the Staff Manual respectively. Title pages will be prepared in manuscript.

Hour, Date, Place	Summary of Events and Information	Remarks and references to Appendices
13th January to 17th January 1916.	During the four days in Brigade Reserve fatigue and working parties were supplied to R.E. and parties were employed keeping communication trenches in repair.	
17th January 1916.	Battalion took over trenches A.7 to A.12 in front line.	
18th January 1916.	Mist prevented any activity during yesterday. 17th Enemy bombarded sector occupied by the Battalion commencing 9.0 a.m. 18th.	
19th January 1916.	Enemy bombarded our trenches from 9.0 a.m. till 11-30 a.m. and 11-55 a.m. till 12.30 p.m. today with whizzbangs and crumps. Casualties 1 man killed, 1 man slightly wounded.	
21st January 1916.	Battalion relieved and proceeded to DICKEBUSCH Huts.	
21st to 25th January 1916.	Battalion in Divisional Reserve at DICKEBUSCH Huts.	
25th January 1916. 26th January 1916.	Battalion took over trenches A.7 to A.12. Patrol from A.12 last night reported that our wire was in good condition and that the enemy appear to be working on the wire between his front and second lines. A green flare was seen well away on our left about 2.30 a.m. Nothing resulted.	
27th January 1916.	A patrol from the right of A.7. proceeded down a ditch and about 100 yards out discovered a wire running across a road, to which was attached a bomb in a hedge beside the ditch. The bomb was bell-shaped with a handle about a foot long.	
29th January 1916.	Flares from the enemy were more numerous. Enemy sent up many flares during last night and also threw bombs in front of his own wire. Nothing to report.	

Army Form C. 2118.

WAR DIARY
or
INTELLIGENCE SUMMARY.
(Erase heading not required.)

Instructions regarding War Diaries and Intelligence Summaries are contained in F.S. Regs., Part II. and the Staff Manual respectively. Title pages will be prepared in manuscript.

Hour, Date, Place	Summary of Events and Information	Remarks and references to Appendices
30th January 1916.	Nothing of importance. Message received that No. 12796 Corpl. Andrew JENKINSON had been awarded the D.C.M. for conspicuous gallantry and devotion to duty in getting wounded away during the bombardment of 10th January 1916. During this tour in the trenches the enemy has been at work on a new forward fire trench.	APPENDIX E. AMENDED TO DATE ATTACHED

/5 Border Regt

Army Form C. 2118.

WAR DIARY
or
INTELLIGENCE SUMMARY.
(Erase heading not required.)

Instructions regarding War Diaries and Intelligence Summaries are contained in F.S. Regs., Part II. and the Staff Manual respectively. Title pages will be prepared in manuscript.

Hour, Date, Place	Summary of Events and Information	Remarks and references to Appendices
3rd February 1916.	On February 3rd message received that 1265 Sgt PAGAN and 1490 L/Cpl. MARTIN, G.S. had been awarded the D.C.M. for conspicuous gallantry in laying wires between Company and Battalion Headquarters during a heavy bombardment on 19th January 1916 involving taking wires across the open.	
12th February 1916.	Captain. R.C.R.Blair reports as follows on a patrol which went out to examine the new enemy forward trench before mentioned :- "Last night at 9.0 p.m. our patrol of 2 Officers and 10 men went out from No.14 Bay. A8 Fire Trench across to the new German trench. We found the trench occupied. Before the enemy who did not now note I looked over into their trench which is about four feet deep and appears to take the rough form of a new fire trench. The enemy ran both ways, some into the wood and some along the trench, and they immediately lit what appeared to be a magnesium powder light. Unfortunately the large portion of my men did not come up alongside of me as arranged or we should have captured a few of the enemy before they got into the wood. I did not follow the enemy up as the position as to unknown ground and the likelihood of accidental shooting from my own men seemed very probable owing to the way they had got bunched up. I should also like to point out that while crossing the opening between the trenches our own guns threw shrapnel over us, which did not tend to help matters. We returned with hardly a shot being fired. It would be worth while sending say 50 men out and take this trench from the enemy or they will soon wire it."	

Forms/C. 2118/10

WAR DIARY
or
INTELLIGENCE SUMMARY.
(Erase heading not required.)

Army Form C. 2118.

Instructions regarding War Diaries and Intelligence Summaries are contained in F.S. Regs., Part II. and the Staff Manual respectively. Title pages will be prepared in manuscript.

Hour, Date, Place	Summary of Events and Information	Remarks and references to Appendices
12th February 1916.	On the night of 12/13th February the Battalion was relieved in the trenches and came out for Brigade rest of 6 days. Owing to the recent hard spell in the trenches the Brigadier General decided that the proposed Brigade training should be abandoned and that the men be rested as much as possible.	
14th February 1916.	Following message received 6-10 p.m. 14/2/16 begins:- "5th Border. Sqr. 14th aaa. 50th Division begins aaa 2nd Division have received S.O.S. from HOOGE and are standing to aaa. 151st Brigade to be prepared to move if called upon at half an hours notice. aaa Horses not to be hitched to aaa 151st Inf. Bde. ends. Following received 7-45 p.m. 14/2/16. begins 5th Border S.CX14. aaa 14th aaa Horses to be harnessed at once but not limbered up. aaa 151st Bde. Bde. On the night 18/19th February the Battalion relieved 5th Yorks Regt. in close support and were distributed as follows:- Battalion H.Q. - SQUARE WOOD. "C" Coy - GLASGOW CROSS "D" " - Supporting in X Trench "A" " - SUNKEN ROAD. "B" " - LARCH WOOD. The two latter Companies supporting the right sector of the Brigade.	
18th February 1916.		

50

1/5 Border Regt

Vol VI

151 Bde

Army Form C. 2118.

WAR DIARY
or
INTELLIGENCE SUMMARY.
(Erase heading not required.)

Instructions regarding War Diaries and Intelligence Summaries are contained in F.S. Regs., Part II. and the Staff Manual respectively. Title pages will be prepared in manuscript.

Hour, Date, Place	Summary of Events and Information	Remarks and references to Appendices
22/2/16.	Much good work was put in by Battalion Grenadiers in cup (Trench 47). Enemy bombers were silenced on every occasion. Telescopic rifles from the CROW'S NEST did much in keeping down enemy snipers.	
	The Battalion moved into position at MOUNT SORREL on February 22nd in relief of 6th D.L.I. taking over trenches 49 to A.3 inclusive. Heavy snow fell during this period and made all attempts at patrolling most difficult; notwithstanding this and other difficulties a considerable amount of work was put out and the position in other respects strengthened.	
26/2/16.	The Battalion was relieved on February 26th by the 6th D.L.I. and retired into Brigade supports at BEDFORD HOUSE with posts at BLAUWE POORT FARM and SWAN CHATEAU.	
29/2/16.	On 29th February Battalion Headquarters "A" & "C" Coys moved to ARMAGH WOOD with 6 platoons to BLAUWEPOORT FARM and 2 to RAILWAY DUGOUTS in close support of MOUNT SORREL. The Battalion remained in this position during the attack made by the 17th Division on enemy line at	
2/3/16.	INTERNATIONAL TRENCH on the morning of 2nd March. The enemy counter-attacked the position won, and under a heavy artillery bombardment four platoons of the Battalion were ordered to reinforce the 9th DUKE OF WELLINGTON'S REGT in trenches. These 2 platoons of "B" Coy and two platoons of "D" Company under the command of Captain WEBB advanced from BLAUWEPOORT FARM through the artillery barrage and took up position. The good work done by this Company was acknowledged by the Divisional Commander and O.C. 9th Duke of Wellington's Regt. (Copy of letters attached.)	APPENDIX "F"

SECRET.

D.A.G.
3rd Echelon.

Herewith War Diary of this Battalion for the month of March 1916.

H. Martin
Adjutant for O.C. 5th Bn. Border Regt.
Lieutenant

Army Form C. 2118.

WAR DIARY
or
INTELLIGENCE SUMMARY.
(Erase heading not required.)

Instructions regarding War Diaries and Intelligence Summaries are contained in F.S. Regs, Part II. and the Staff Manual respectively. Title pages will be prepared in manuscript.

Hour, Date, Place	Summary of Events and Information	Remarks and references to Appendices
6/3/16.	The Battalion was relieved by the 6th D.L.I. on 6th March and returned to billets at CANADA HUTS, DICKEBUSCH. Heavy snow fell during the rest period.	Casualties 18/2/16 to 6/3/16:- D.R. KILLED 1 . 3 WOUNDED - 11
9/3/16.	The Battalion remained under orders to be ready to reinforce at 2 hours notice until the 9th March when the situation having cleared, the order was cancelled. The Battalion relieved the 8th Bn D.L.I. on the night of 12th March - H.Q. and "A" Coy at ARMAGH WOOD, "C" Coy at H.20 (sheet 28) "D" Coy and half "B" Coy at BLAUWEPOORT FARM, half of "B" Coy at Railway dugouts, in support of 6th Bn. Northumberland Fusiliers. Considerable artillery activity on both sides during this period.	
14/3/16.	On the night of 14th March the Battalion moved into the front line - H.Q. at SQUARE WOOD, "A" Company GLASGOW CROSS, "B" Company LARCH WOOD and R.7. "C" Company X Trench, "D" Company trenches 41, 41/S and 47/S. During the four days in the above area the enemy fired a lot of rifle grenades, aircraft and trench mortars into our trenches, but our replies always silenced him and he did very little damage.	
18/3/16.	On the night of 18th March the Battalion was relieved by the 4th Yorkshire Regiment and was railed from GOLDFISH CHATEAU (H.11 centre. sheet 28) to relief billets in POPERINGHE. Battalion remained under orders to reinforce at three hours notice during the rest period.	

WAR DIARY
or
INTELLIGENCE SUMMARY.

(Erase heading not required.)

Army Form C. 2118.

Hour, Date, Place	Summary of Events and Information	Remarks and references to Appendices
20/3/16.	A Court of Enquiry was held on 20/3/16. (President:- Capt. A.B. Cockburn. Members Lt. F.W. Glass and Lieut. Murtha Lagan. A.J. Ford) on Iron rations on Battalion charge. The Court recommended that the grocery portion of the ration, which had deteriorated, be renewed, and 550 rations were asked for and obtained.	
23/3/16.	On the night of 23rd March the Battalion took over trenches 32, 33 and 34 from the 8th Bn. The King's Own Regiment, distribution as follows:- "A" Coy. Trench 32. "B" " Trench 33 "C" " Trench 34 "D" " Trenches 32 and 33 Supports.	
24/3/16.	On the 24th the enemy shelled BLAUWEPOORT FARM with H.E. and on the 25th he Whizz-banged the RAVINE and Battalion Headquarters. In neither case did he do any damage. Enemy snipers are kept well in hand on this front and are not causing so much trouble as is usually the case.	
27/3/16.	At about 4.15 a.m. on the morning of the 27th a mine appeared to have been exploded about a mile to the south. This was followed by a heavy bombardment, our guns doing most of the work. On the night of the 27th/28th March "A", "C" and "D" Coys and Lewis Gunners were relieved by the 7th Bn. D.L.I.	

Army Form C. 2118.

WAR DIARY
or
INTELLIGENCE SUMMARY.
(Erase heading not required.)

Instructions regarding War Diaries and Intelligence Summaries are contained in F.S. Regs., Part II. and the Staff Manual respectively. Title pages will be prepared in manuscript.

Hour, Date, Place	Summary of Events and Information	Remarks and references to Appendices
27/3/16	"B" Company being temporarily attached to the 7th Bn. D.L.I. to complete the position. Headquarters and three Companies moved to WOODCOTE HOUSE in Brigade Reserve.	
29/3/16	"B" Company were relieved by "C" Company in 325 Trench on 29th and Headquarters, "A", "B" and "D" Companies moved to BEDFORD HOUSE.	
31/3/16	On 31/3/16 the Battalion relieved the 7th Bn. D.L.I. and Companies were distributed as follows:— "A" Coy. Trench 32. "D" " Trench 33. "C" " from Trench 325 to Trench 34 "B" " to Supports.	

APPENDIX F

C O P Y.

To O.C. 5th Bn The Border Regiment.
————————————————

Dear Sir,

Please accept my thanks and appreciation for the four platoons of your Regiment that came to reinforce my Battalion on March 2nd.

Your men were splendid. They came through the barrage in perfect order and behaved throughout with great gallantry.

I hope your losses were not too severe.

My men much appreciate your help.

     Yours sincerely,

      (Sd) G.E.WANNELL, Major,

6/3/16.   O.C. 9th Duke of Wellington's Regiment.

C O P Y.

Dear Shea,

General Pilcher has written asking me to express his thanks to you, and the Officers of the 5th Borders and 9th D.L.I. concerned, for the quick and ready manner in which assistance was rendered to the 9th Duke of Wellington's Regiment on 2nd March when they were hard put to it. The Officer Commanding this Battalion informed General Pilcher that the prompt help he received in being sent stores of different descriptions as well as troops was of the greatest value.

Will you let the troops concerned know how their services were appreciated.

Yours sincerely,

(Sd) P.S. WILKINSON.

SECRET.

1/5 Border Regt 50
Vol 4

D.A.G.

    BASE.
    ⎯⎯⎯⎯

    Herewith War Diary of this Battalion for April, 1916, also Appendix 'C', to date.

                                   J.R. Hedley   Lieut.Colonel,

15/5/16.   Commanding, 5th Bn The Border Regiment.

Army Form C. 2118.

WAR DIARY
or
INTELLIGENCE SUMMARY.
(Erase heading not required.)

Instructions regarding War Diaries and Intelligence Summaries are contained in F.S. Regs., Part II. and the Staff Manual respectively. Title pages will be prepared in manuscript.

Hour, Date, Place	Summary of Events and Information	Remarks and references to Appendices
2/4/16.	Nothing of interest occurred during this tour and on the night 2/3rd April the Battalion was relieved by the 1st and 2nd Canadian Battalions and moved to Canada Huts.	
4/4/16.	On the 4th April the Battalion relieved the 27th Battalion Canadian in trenches N.3, N.4, N.5, N.6, O.1, O.1A, O.2, O.3, O.4. S.P.7. Eastern Redoubt and Western Redoubt.	
6, 7th & 8th /4/16.	On the 6th, 7th and 8th April there was much activity on our immediate left held by the Canadians and the Craters in front of St. Eloi changed hands several times. "C" Company who were on the left received the edge of the enemy's shelling but casualties were not severe, though our parapet was breached in several places.	
8/4/16.	On the 8th April the Battalion was relieved by the 6th Br. Durham Light Infantry and moved into Brigade reserve at RIDGEWOOD (N.3. a.Sheet 28).	
8/4/16 to 11/4/16.	During the three days in RIDGEWOOD the enemy shelled continually searching for our Batteries in the vicinity. Large working parties were supplied for repairing trenches and support lines each night.	
11/4/16.	On the night of the 11th April, the Battalion was relieved by the 9th Br. Durham Light Infantry and occupied billets at LA CLYTTE (Divisional Reserve).	
14/4/16.	On the 14th April 1916 the Battalion relieved the 8th Br. Durham Light Infantry in the Right Sector, occupying trenches M.1, M.2, N.2, N.2.a, N.3 (Three Companies) with Battalion Headquarters and one Company near VIERSTRAAT. Practically the whole time the Battalion occupied this position, the enemy shelled trenches M.1, and M.2, evidently	

WAR DIARY or INTELLIGENCE SUMMARY.

(Erase heading not required.)

Army Form C. 2118.

Hour, Date, Place	Summary of Events and Information	Remarks and references to Appendices
17/4/16	Working for our mine shaft which is near. On one occasion they succeeded in placing a shell directly in the mouth of the shaft. Trenches were breached in several places, but were repaired by working parties at night. On the night of the 17th "C" Company who had been in support, relieved "A" Company in trenches M.1, and M.2. During the time the Battalion was in the area occupied from 3/4/16 to present date, it has been found most difficult to carry out reliefs, or to bring up stores expeditiously owing to the fact that there are only two communication trenches in this sector namely, the Pt. O. C.T. and the CHICORY C.T. Owing to heavy bombardment the Pand.Q was impassable almost the whole time.	
20/4/16	The Battalion was relieved by the 8th Bn Durham Light on 20/4/16 and proceeded to rest billets at LACLYTTE. Captain R.C.R.Blair D.S.O. proceeded to the War Office to attend a munitions conference held on 22/4/16.	
21/4/16	Battalion marched from billets near LACLYTTE to an area about one mile east of BERTHEN. Companies in farms within 1,000 yards of Headquarters.	
21/4/16 to 30/4/16	From 21st April to 30th April, Battalion spent time in inspections, refitting clothing and equipment, overhauling stores and transport. Individual training commenced and various courses of instruction started. The Battalion was inspected by General Sir Douglas Haig. G.O.C. in C. British Army in the Field, on 29/4/16.	

5TH BATTALION THE BORDER REGIMENT.

Particulars of Officers.

Officers who came to France 25/10/14.

Lieut.Col T.A.Milburn	Invalided to England, 25/7/15
Major A.C.Scoular.	Invalided to England, 23/3/15.
Major A.D.Soulsby,	Temp. Lieut.Colonel 28/3/15. Temp. Major 11/11/15.
Captain A.F.Broadley-Smith.	Temp. Major 18/4/15. Killed in action 16/6/15.
Captain H.J.Bewlay.	Temp. Major 17/6/15. To England 22/2/16.
Captain R.C.R.Blair, DSO.	To England (W.O.Special leave) 21/10/15. Rejoined Battn. 2/2/16.
Captain S.Rigg.	To England 15/9/15. Rejoined Battalion 25/4/16.
Captain W.F.Spedding.	To England 3/6/15. Rejoined Battalion 9/8/15. To England 7/1/16.
Captain H.R.Petts.	To England 26/12/15.
Captain A.B.Cowburn.	
Captain E.A.Iredale.	
Lieut. H.C.Webb.	Temp. Captain 18/4/15. To England 26/5/15. Rejoined Battalion 7/7/15.
Lieut. J.W.Robinson	Temp.Captain 18/6/15. To England 29/6/15. Rejoined Battalion 7/10/15.
Lieut. W.Adair.	To England 12/3/16.
Lieut. W.S.Sewell.	To England 20/5/15. Rejoined Battalion 7/10/15.
Lieut. R.J.Rice.	Temp. Captain 16/6/15. Wounded 3/7/15. To England 22/8/15.
Lieut. F.B.Spedding.	To England 15/8/15. Rejoined Battalion 25/4/16.
Lieut. C.N. Jenkins.	To Base duty and struck off strength 29/12/15.
Lieut. F.P.Longmire.	To England 10/5/15. Rejoined Battalion 25/4/16.
2/Lieut. C.Graham.	Temp. Lieut. 18/4/15. Killed in action 27/5/15.
2/Lieut. G.G.Askew.	Wounded 6/7/15. To England 13/7/15. Rejoined 25/4/16.

2.

Officers who came to France, 25/10/14 (continued).

2/Lieut. J.N.Franks.	To England 20/3/15. Rejoined Battalion 1/1/16.
2/Lieut. H.P.Smith.	Wounded 23/5/15. To England 27/5/15. Rejoined Battalion 25/4/16.
2/Lieut. J.B.McGhie.	To England, 30/4/15. Rejoined Battalion 19/12/15.
2/Lieut. I.H.M.Humphreys.	Wounded 12/6/15. To England 27/6/15.
2/Lieut. P.W.Maclagan.	Killed in action 16/4/16.
Major & Quartermaster G.Pecker.	To England 17/1/16.
Captain & Adjutant T.W.MacDonald.	To England 20/6/15.
Chaplain & Hon.Lt.Col.Campbell.	To England 27/12/14.
Lieut. W.Marley Cass, RAMC. Att.	To England 20/2/15.

Joined 17/12/14.

2/Lieut. J.W.Adair.   Wounded 17/5/15. To England 27/5/15.

Joined 9/1/15.

2/Lt. W.F.D. de La Touche.   Wounded 24/5/15. To England 21/7/15.

Joined 12/7/15.

2/Lieut. W.P.Bennett.	Temp.Lieut. 18/7/15. Att. 151/1 Trench Mortar Battery. Wounded 21/4/16.
2/Lieut. H.Bennett.	To England 15/8/15.
2/Lieut. H.E.Wood.	Temp.Lieut. 6/8/15. To 151st Brigade MG. Coy.(Seconded) 6/2/16.
2/Lieut. P.B.C.Holdsworth.	Wounded 14/7/15. To England 25/7/15.
2/Lieut. A.S.Wilson.	Wounded 25/9/15. To England 29/9/15. Rejoined Battalion 31/1/16.
2/Lieut. C.K.Montgomery.	To England 5/12/15.
2/Lieut. D.W.Glass.	a/Adjutant 29/7/15. To duty 12/2/16.
2/Lieut. J.M.Main.	Seconded for duty with 182nd Tunnelling Coy, R.E. 2/10/15.
2/Lieut. R.B.Oliver.	Brigade Bombing Officer, 151st. Inf. Bde.
2/Lieut. O.J.Feetham.	
2/Lieut. J.R.Percy.	Wounded 17/7/15. To England 22/7/15. Rejoined Battalion 7/10/15.

3.

Joined 13/7/15.

  2/Lieut. R.W.Marley.   Temp. Lieut. 26/6/15. To 151st Inf. Bde
                                       M.G.Coy (Seconded) 6/2/16. To
                                       England 20/4/16.

Joined 30/7/15.

  2/Lieut. L.Ewbank.   Killed in action 23/3/16.

~~Joined 8/8/15.~~   Commissioned from ranks of this Battalion.

  2/Lieut. C.E.Pass.   Proceeded to join 2/5th Border Regt 10/9/15.
                                       Rejoined Battalion 3/3/16.

Joined 22/9/15. from 5th Royal Berks. Regt as Commanding Officer.

  Major W.R.P.Kemmis-Betty.   To England 26/10/15.

Joined 6/10/15.

  Lieut. G.J.Monsen-Fitzjohn. To R.F.C. 16/1/16. Seconded 11/3/16.

Joined 1/11/15.

  2/Lieut. H.P.Rhind.   To England 11/3/16.

Joined 2/11/15.

  2/Lieut. G.Hill.   To England 15/1/16.

Joined 11/11/15. from 6th Bn North'd Fusrs. as Commanding Officer.

  Major J.R.Hedley.   Temp. Lieut.Colonel 11/11/15.

Joined 24/12/15.

  2/Lieut. J.A.Stout.

Joined 8/1/16.

  2/Lieut. G.H.Dawes.

Joined 12/2/16. from The Royal Scots as Adjutant.

  Lieut. J.H.Martin.

Joined 13/2/16.

  2/Lieut. J.P.Bennett.

Joined 14/2/16.

   2/Lieut. A.L.Ford.

   2/Lieut. A.G.Condi.

Joined 16/3/16.

   2/Lieut. C.R.Suiter.

Joined 8/5/16.   From Cadets' School, G.H.Q.

   2/Lieut. J.Mackay.

   2/Lieut. E.J.Pursglove.

   2/Lieut. J.S.Booth.

Joined 11/5/16.

   2/Lieut. H.B.Beaumont.

Joined 12/5/16.

   2/Lieut. H.Bell.

WAR DIARY
or
INTELLIGENCE SUMMARY.
(Erase heading not required.)

Army Form C. 2118.

1/5 Bucks Regt
A I & I

Hour, Date, Place	Summary of Events and Information	Remarks and References to Appendices
23-5-16	The Division was inspected at FRETRE by General Sir Herbert C.O. Plumer, G.C.M.G., K.C.B. Commanding Second Army, who decorated a large number of all ranks for gallantry in the field. The Division afterwards "Marched Passed", the Divisional Band playing the various Regimental Marches.	
24-5-16	The following message was received, headed:- Army Commander's Message of appreciation:- The Commander, Second Army, on presenting Medals to the Division on the 23rd May, 1916 wishes the following message to be conveyed to all ranks:- He was very glad of the opportunity of inspecting the Division, and much pleased with their turnout and appearance, he complimented the Division on its consistent good work in this country since the first week of its landing up to the present time. While congratulating those to whom he had presented Medals on this occasion he quite recognize that they are only a	

WAR DIARY
or
INTELLIGENCE SUMMARY.
(Erase heading not required.)

Army Form C. 2118.

Instructions regarding War Diaries and Intelligence Summaries are contained in F. S. Regs., Part II. and the Staff Manual respectively. Title pages will be prepared in manuscript.

Hour, Date, Place	Summary of Events and Information	Remarks and References to Appendices
25-5-16	type of the Division as a whole and that many more acts of equal devotion and gallantry have been performed by those who have gone unrewarded. From the 21st April to the 25th May the Bn. went through systematic training and individual Courses of Instruction including a Riding Course for Young Officers. At about 4.15 p.m. on the 25th May, a bombing accident took place in the Bn. Bombing Pit, causing twenty casualties, five men dying from the wounds. Three Officer were wounded, Lieut. J.P. Bennett, Lieut. J. Mackay, and Lieut L.O. Stocken, attached from 10th Middlesex Regiment.	
26-5-16	The Bn. Left its Rest Area for LA CLYTTE, via WESTOUTRE, parading at 8.0 a.m. and billeted in huts in the Divisional Reserve Area. The Bombers, Lewis Gunners and Snipers proceeded to the trenches tonight, and relieved their respective sections of the 2nd Bn. The Royal Scots.	
27-5-16	Final preparations for trenches tonight. The Bn. paraded at	

Army Form C. 2118.

WAR DIARY
or
INTELLIGENCE SUMMARY.
(Erase heading not required.)

Hour, Date, Place	Summary of Events and Information	Remarks and References to Appendices
	7.15 p.m. and moved off in the following order, "D", "C", "B", "A" Coy. with five minute intervals between companies, and relieved the 2nd Bn. The Royal Scots in the Right Sub Sector of the Brigade frontage, "D" Coy taking over the garrison at VIERSTRAAT. The Bn. frontage consists of Trenches M.1, M.2, M.3, N.1, N.2, N.2a., Bn. H.d. being in RIDGEWOOD.	The following extracts appeared in the London Gazette, 3/2-6/16 Major (Temp. Lt. Col.) JOHN RALPH HEDLEY Northbn. Huss. T.F. Commdg. In. Bn. Border Rgt. to be companion of the DISTINGUISHED SERVICE ORDER
3.6.16	Nothing of interest occurred during this day of duty in the trenches beyond a considerable amount of aircraft activity. The enemy mostly confined himself to the use of Trench Mortars and Rifle Grenades. Practically no casualties occurred and on the night of the 2/3rd. of June the Bn. was relieved by 9th 8th Bn. Durham L.I. and moved into Bde. Reserve in RIDGEWOOD (N.3.a. She 28) Awarded the MILITARY MEDAL. Nothing of interest occurred during the six days the Bn. spent in RIDGEWOOD beyond the fact that during to the Bn. being so weak almost everyman was taken nightly for working parties.	271 Sjt. (A/C.S.M.) AITKEN, T. Awarded the DISTINGUISHED CONDUCT MEDAL. 755 Pte. WILSON G.
7.6.16	The Lewis Guns relieved the Lewis Guns of the 8th Bn. Durham L.I. in the	

WAR DIARY
or
INTELLIGENCE SUMMARY.
(Erase heading not required.)

Army Form C. 2118.

Hour, Date, Place	Summary of Events and Information	Remarks and References to Appendices
8.6.16	Right Sub Sector tonight. The Bn. relieved the 9th Bn. in the Right Sub Sector, Sub Units relieved during daylight. Coys. parading at 7.30 p.m. and moving at intervals in the following order, "C", "D", "A". Leaving "B" Company to form the garrison at VERSTRAAT Bn. H.Q. remained in RIDGEWOOD.	
11.6.16	The enemy has kept up this activity with trench Mortars and Rifle Grenades but so far has done little damage. This morning at 2.30 the enemy exploded a mine at N.12.d.3.1. sheet 28, and in occupying the "Crater" had to expose himself, our Lewis Guns under 1619 Corporal D. Macan taking heavy toll. The mine was exploded in the enemy's own lines and the enemy appeared dazed with the shock and the understachme appeared up an undermined fire on the enemy Support + Reserve lines. The enemy retaliated weakly on M.1 + 2 trenches but did no damage. During the night one of our Patrols heard the

WAR DIARY
or
INTELLIGENCE SUMMARY.
(Erase heading not required.)

Army Form C. 2118.

Instructions regarding War Diaries and Intelligence Summaries are contained in F. S. Regs., Part II. and the Staff Manual respectively. Title pages will be prepared in manuscript.

Hour, Date, Place	Summary of Events and Information	Remarks and References to Appendices
12.6.16	sound of grass being cut, whereupon our Lewis Guns opened fire. Several Boche Corpses were observed next morning. Our Snipers secured three men during the day.	
	A small bombing party under Lieut. J.R. Franks went from M.1. last night and reached the new crater, they threw in a dozen Mills Bombs and retired in order to be back by 11.0 p.m. when the heavies were due to fire in retaliation. The enemy merely threw over four rifle Grenades which fell behind our trenches.	
13.6.16	At 4.0 p.m. the enemy started on M.1., M.2. and N.1. with "Rum Jars" (T.M.) and later with 5.9" Crumps & Wooly Bears which caused no four casualties, and kept it up for half an hour when our artillery silenced him. During the last 8 days the Intelligence did exceptionally good work. The Lewis Guns were relieved tonight by the 8th Bn. Durham L.I.	
14.6.16	At various times during the day the enemy in retaliation for our artillery, got very active with trench mortars, Crumps	

WAR DIARY or INTELLIGENCE SUMMARY.

(Erase heading not required.)

Army Form C. 2118.

Instructions regarding War Diaries and Intelligence Summaries are contained in F.S. Regs., Part II. and the Staff Manual respectively. Title pages will be prepared in manuscript.

Hour, Date, Place	Summary of Events and Information	Remarks and References to Appendices
15-6-16	Whizz-bangs over Mr. & Mr. 2 and heavily shrapnelled Western Redoubt, but quietened down when our artillery heavily bombarded HOLLANDSCHESSHOUR FARM. During this tour we had a fair number of casualties. D'Coy. having the worst. On the night of the 14th/15th June, the Bn. was relieved by the 8th Bn. Durham L.I. and moved into Divisional Reserve at LA CLYTTE. An Officers Mess was started in a big hut, the pioneers erecting tables and forms in the shape of an horse shoe, and was found to be a great success. A Sergeants Mess was also formed, with the same details. British Army-time advanced one hour.	
16-6-16	Baths at LA CLYTTE were allotted to the Bn. for 6 hours which enabled every man to have a bath and change of under-clothing.	
17-6-16	"B""D" Coys. and Sub Units proceeded to BAILLEUL Aerodrome today in order to become acquainted with the various types of machines & used by the Allies on the present front.	
19-6-16	The Lewis Guns relieved the Lewis Guns of the 8th Bn. Durham L.I.	

WAR DIARY
or
INTELLIGENCE SUMMARY.

Instructions regarding War Diaries and Intelligence Summaries are contained in F. S. Regs., Part II. and the Staff Manual respectively. Title pages will be prepared in manuscript.

Army Form C. 2118.

Hour, Date, Place	Summary of Events and Information	Remarks and References to Appendices
	in the right Sub Sector, tonight.	
20-6-16	The C.O. held a kit inspection during the period the Bn. was in Divisional Reserve, the usual short parades and inspections were held and the new method of wearing the "Gas Helmet" was taught.	
	The Bn. relieved the 8th Bn. Durham L.I. in the Right Sub Sector leaving LA CLYTTE at 8.50 pm in the following order: "C", "D", "B" "A" Coys. with five minutes interval between Companies. Sub Units relieved during daylight. "C" Coy. formed the garrison at VIERSTRAAT, Bn. H.Q. being as formerly in RIDGEWOOD.	
23-6-16	Nothing extraordinary has happened so far in this tour of duty, beyond the fact that the enemy has been very active with his Trench Mortars and Rifle Grenades, but inflicting very few casualties and doing little damage	
24-6-16	Our 18 prs. & 4.2" have been crossing the enemy's wire steadily all day, the enemy retaliating with a few Salvoes	

Army Form C. 2118.

WAR DIARY
or
INTELLIGENCE SUMMARY.
(Erase heading not required.)

Instructions regarding War Diaries and Intelligence Summaries are contained in F. S. Regs., Part II. and the Staff Manual respectively. Title pages will be prepared in manuscript.

Hour, Date, Place	Summary of Events and Information	Remarks and References to Appendices
25.6.16	and Trench Mortars but only inflicting one casualty. From the 24th our artillery has been firing steadily at the enemy's trenches and wire. Enemy retaliating on our trenches with T.M.s and Minenwerfer but with little effect.	
26.6.16	The Bn. was relieved on the night of the 26th/27th by the 8th Bn. Durham L.I. relief being rather late owing to the wild, stormy weather and the rain. Sub Units were relieved during daylight. Lewis Guns were relieved on the night of the 25th/26th. Two new Lewis Guns received making a total of Six in the Bn. Lewis Gun position taken up at BRASSERIE while Battalion is in Brigade Reserve at RIDGEWOOD.	
29.6.16	Nothing of interest happened to the Battalion while in RIDGEWOOD. except that every available man is taken up for working parties nightly. Our artillery has been firing heavily on the German Lines for the last few days, an intense engagement taking place at about 12 midnight.	

Forms/C. 2118/11.

Army Form C. 2118.

WAR DIARY
or
INTELLIGENCE SUMMARY.
(Erase heading not required.)

Instructions regarding War Diaries and Intelligence Summaries are contained in F. S. Regs., Part II. and the Staff Manual respectively. Title pages will be prepared in manuscript.

Hour, Date, Place	Summary of Events and Information	Remarks and References to Appendices
	Last night. On our Right. The Great Offensive started today in the South.	

D.A.G.
　　3rd Echelon, G.H.Q.
　　　Base.
==============================

　　　　Herewith APPENDIX "G" and particulars of Officers for
War Diary of this Battalion, please.

　　　　　　　　　　　　　　　　　　　　　　H.P.Smith　Lieutenant,
30/6/16.　　　　　　　a/Adjutant, for O.C.5th Bn. The Border Regiment.

5TH BATTALION THE BORDER REGIMENT.

Particulars of Officers.

Officers who came to France 25/10/14:-

Lieut. Col. T.A.Milburn	Invalided to England, 25/7/15.
Major A.C.Scouler	Invalided to England, 25/3/15.
Major A.D.Soulsby	Temp. Lieut. Colonel 28/8/15. Temp. Major 11/11/15.
Captain A.F.Broadly-Smith	Temp. Major 18/4/15. Killed in action 16/6/16.
Captain H.J.Bewley	Temp. Major 17/6/15. To England 22/2/16.
Captain R.C.R.Blair, D.S.O.	To England (W.O.Special leave) 21/10/15 Rejoined Bn. 2/2/16. To England (W.O. Special leave) 20/4/16 Rejoined Bn. 24/6/16
Captain S.Rigg	To England 15/9/15. Rejoined Bn. 25/4/16.
Captain W.F.Spedding	To England 3/6/15. Rejoined Bn. 9/8/15. To England 7/1/16.
Captain H.R.Potts	To England 26/12/15.
Captain A.B.Cowburn	
Captain E.A.Iredale	
Lieut. H.C.Webb	Temp. Captain 18/4/15. To England 26/5/15. Rejoined Bn. 7/7/15. To Stokes Gun Coy. 27/6/16.
Lieut. J.W.Robinson	Temp. Captain 18/6/15. To England 29/6/15. Rejoined Bn. 7/10/15.
Lieut. W.Adair	To England 12/3/16.
Lieut. W.S.Sewell	To England 20/5/15. Rejoined BN. 7/10/15. TO ENGLAND 22/5/16
Lieut. R.J.Rice	Temp. Captain 16/6/15. Wounded 3/7/15. To England 22/8/15.
Lieut. F.B.Spedding	To England 15/8/15. Rejoined Bn. 25/4/16.
Lieut. C.N.Jenkins	To Base duty and struck off strength 29/12/15.
Lieut. F.P.Longmire	To England 10/5/15. Rejoined Bn. 25/4/16.
2/Lieut. C.Graham	Temp.Lieut. 18/4/15. Killed in action 27/5/15.
2/Lieut. G.G.Askew	Wounded 6/7/15. To England 13/7/15. Rejoined Bn. 25/4/16. TEMP. LIEUT. 18/4/16
2/Lieut. J.N.Franks	To England 20/8/15. Rejoined Bn. 1/1/16. TEMP LIEUTENANT 20/5/15.

(2)

Officers who came to France, 25/10/14, continued.

2/Lieut. H.P.Smith	Wounded 24/5/15. To England 27/5/15. Rejoined Bn. 25/4/16. Temp. Lieut.19/4/15.
2/Lieut. J.B.McGhie	To England 30/4/15. Rejoined Bn. 19/12/15.
2/Lieut. I.H.M.Humphreys	Wounded 12/6/15. To England 27/6/15.
2/Lieut. P.W.Maclagan	Temp. Lieut.27/5/15. Killed in action 16/4/16.
Major & Qr. Mr. G.Pecker	To England 13/1/16.
Captain & Adj. T.W.MacDonald	To England 20/6/15.
Chaplain & Hon.Lt.Col.Campbell	To England 27/12/14.
Lieut. W.Marley Gass, RAMC att.	To England 20/2/15.

Joined Bn. 17/12/14.

2/Lieut. J.W.Adair	Wounded 17/5/15. To England 27/5/15.

Joined Bn. 9/1/15.

2/Lt. W.F.D. de la Touche	Wounded 24/5/15. To England 21/7/15.

Joined Bn. 12/7/15.

2/Lieut. W.P.Bennett	Temp. Lieut. 13/7/15. Att. 151/1 Trench Mortar Battery. Wounded 21/4/15. To England 4/5/16.
2/Lieut. H.Bennett	To England 15/8/15.
2/Lieut. H.E.Wood	Temp.Lieut. 6/8/15. To 151st Inf.Bde. M.G. Coy.(Seconded) 6/2/16.
2/Lieut. P.B.C.Holdsworth	Wounded 14/7/15. To England 23/7/15.
2/Lieut. A.S.Wilson	Wounded 25/9/15. To England 29/9/15. Rejoined Bn. 31/1/16.
2/Lieut. C.K.Montgomery	To England 5/12/15.
2/Lieut. D.W.Glass	a/Adjutant 29/7/15. To duty 12/2/16.
2/Lieut. J.M.Main	Seconded for duty with 182nd Tunnelling Coy, R.E. 2/10/15.
2/Lieut. R.B.Oliver	151st Inf. Bde Bombing Officer.
2/Lieut. O.J.Feetham	
2/Lieut. J.R.Percy	Wounded 17/7/15. To England 22/7/15. Rejoined Bn. 7/10/15.

(3)

Joined Bn. 13/7/15.
2/Lieut. R.W.Marley — Temp. Lieut. 26/6/15. To 151st Inf. Bde. M.G.Coy. (Seconded) 6/2/16. To England 20/4/16.

Joined Bn. 30/7/15.
2/Lieut. L.Ewbank — Killed in action 23/2/16.

Commissioned from ranks of this Battalion.
2/Lieut. C.E.Pass — Proceeded to join 2/5th Bn. Border Regiment 10/9/15. Rejoined Bn. 3/3/16.

Joined Bn. 22/9/15. from 5th Royal Berks. Regt. as Commanding Officer.
Major W.R.P.Kemmis-Betty — To England 26/10/15.

Joined Bn. 6/10/15.
Lieut. G.J.Monson-Fitzjohn — To R.F.C. 16/1/16. Seconded 11/3/16.

Joined Bn. 1/11/15.
2/Lieut. H.P.Rhind — To England 11/3/16.

Joined Bn. 2/11/15.
2/Lieut. G.Hill — To England 15/1/16.

Joined Bn. 11/11/15. from 6th Bn. North'bn Fusrs. as Commanding Officer
Major J.R.Hedley, D.S.O. — Temp Lieut.Colonel 11/11/15.

Joined Bn. 24/12/15.
2/Lieut. J.A.Stout

Joined Bn. 8/1/16.
2/Lieut. G.H.Dawes

Joined Bn. 12/2/16. from 2nd Bn. Royal Scots as Adjutant.
Lieut. J.H.Martin.

Joined Bn. 13/2/16.
2/Lieut. J.P.Bennett — Wounded 25/5/16. To England 1/6/16.

Joined Bn. 14/2/16.
2/Lieut. A.L.Ford
2/Lieut. A.G.Gondi

(4)

<u>Joined Bn. 16/5/16.</u>

2/Lieut. C.R.Suiter   To Trench Mortar Battery 25/5/16.

<u>Joined Bn. 8/5/16.</u>   from Cadet School, G.H.Q.

2/Lieut. J.Mackay   Wounded 25/5/16. To England 5/6/16.

2/Lieut. E.J.Pursglove   Wounded 1/6/16. To England 4/6/16.

2/Lieut. J.S.Booth

<u>Joined Bn. 11/5/16.</u>

2/Lieut. H.B.Beaumont

<u>Joined Bn. 12/5/16.</u>

2/Lieut. H.Bell

<u>Joined Bn. 18/5/16.</u>   10th Middlesex Regt.(attached)

2/Lieut. H. Pride

2/Lieut. L.O.Stocken   Wounded 25/5/16. To England 4/6/16.

<u>Joined Bn. 19/5/16.</u>

2/Lieut. A.Feetham
2/Lieut. H.Hutchinson

<u>Joined Bn. 2/6/16.</u>

Lt.& Qr.Mr. M.Davies.

<u>Joined Bn. 5/6/16.</u>

2/Lieut. C.W.Fagan

<u>Joined Bn. 10/6/16.</u>

2/Lieut. F.J.Lain
2/Lieut. S.E.MacGowan

<u>Joined Bn. 12/6/16.</u>

2/Lieut. J.H.E.Coombes
2/Lieut. R.P.Baxter.

<u>Joined Bn. 25/6/16.</u>

2/Lieut. F.S.Marchant
2/Lieut. J.Huntington

Army Form C. 2118.

WAR DIARY
or
INTELLIGENCE SUMMARY

(Erase heading not required.)

Instructions regarding War Diaries and Intelligence Summaries are contained in F. S. Regs., Part II. and the Staff Manual respectively. Title Pages will be prepared in manuscript.

Place	Date	Hour	Summary of Events and Information	Remarks and references to Appendices

Vol 10

5th Bn. The Border Regt.
War Diary.
July, 1916.
Volume No. 24

Army Form C. 2118.

WAR DIARY
or
INTELLIGENCE SUMMARY.
(Erase heading not required.)

Instructions regarding War Diaries and Intelligence Summaries are contained in F. S. Regs., Part II. and the Staff Manual respectively. Title pages will be prepared in manuscript.

Place	Date	Hour	Summary of Events and Information	Remarks and references to Appendices
	30.6.16		A draft of 62 O.R. joined the Battalion at Ridgewood at 5.30 p.m. Possibly they had come under the enemy observation on the way up, for immediately on their arrival 10 heavy shells fell in the wood wounding four of the draft, one of whom died about two hours afterwards.	
	1.7.16		Ridgewood was again shelled about 6 p.m. five shells being distributed over the wood without doing any damage. The Battalion relieved the 8th Bn. DURHAM LIGHT INFY. in the evening in trenches N.1.2.3. and N.1.2.7.2.A. taking over new Bn. H.Q. at Vierstraat.	
MGN. TRENCHES	2.7.16		The day passed quietly, being disturbed only by a few trench mortar bombs which struck the parapet in one place, but caused no other damage.	
	3.7.16		An officer's patrol under Lt. JN. FRANKS went out during the night 2nd - 3rd from M.1. French and on returning reported sounds of work on enemy's parapet. Lewis Guns were fired on and caused the work to cease. Enemy's front line trenches in the HOLLANDSCHESCHUUR SALIENT show much evidence of battering by our Artillery.	
	4.7.16		Enemy Artillery and French Mortars quiet. Our guns fired at intervals on	

T2M4. Wt. W708-776. 500000. 4/15. Sir J. C. & S.

Army Form C. 2118.

WAR DIARY
or
INTELLIGENCE SUMMARY.
(Erase heading not required.)

Place	Date	Hour	Summary of Events and Information	Remarks and references to Appendices
M4M. TRENCHES	4/7/16		Craters, front line & Supports. Grand Bois & Bois Quarante. Our Lewis Guns played on enemy front line and wire to prevent work. Rifle Grenades were also used for same purpose.	
		9.30 P.m.	Enemy Aeroplanes flew over Dickebusch & Ridgewood, VOORMEZEELE & VIERSTRAAT: and dropped two bombs in open country behind Ridgewood.	
		9.30 P.m.	Enemy Aeroplane returning dropped 3 Signal lights on crossing the German lines, probably to announce its nationality to the German Gunners. Breaches in parapet exposed a system of what appeared power wires entering the German Front Line Trench near the Hollandsschuur Crater (N.12.d.3.1. Sheet 28) and there was much speculation as to the purpose for which they were there. The system appeared to be a renewal of one noticed at same spot about the end of June which was then destroyed by our artillery.	
	5.7.16		During night of 4th/5th. Officers patrol went out from M.I. (2/Lt. FAGAN) & N.2.ª (Capt. BLAIR D.S.O.) and reported no sign of enemy patrols, but sounds of work indicated great activity in the repair of the enemy trenches. Enemy snipers have shown more activity yesterday and today using dummies &	

WAR DIARY or INTELLIGENCE SUMMARY

Army Form C. 2118.

Place	Date	Hour	Summary of Events and Information	Remarks and references to Appendices
	6.7.16		devices for attracting attention, then firing periscopes at our periscopes. This change of attitude seems to point to a relief having taken place two days ago. Transport shelled at Kemmel at Vierstraat at 11:30 p.m. (No casualties).	
			Artillery. Both enemy towers active on the front of Brigade on our Right. K. & L. Trenches and registered with howitzers on support lines of M & N Trenches.	
	7.7.16		Enemy Artillery quiet, only a dozen or so shells falling within our area. Our heavy guns in the vicinity of Kemmel placed half-a-dozen shells in region of N.18.b.7½.9. (Sheet 28) to demolish new works recently constructed at that front. Enemy Snipers busy firing at our periscopes during the day, while at night sentries or fixed rifles fired steadily at our parapets. Our snipers got two hits including an Officer. Several Germans observed looking over parapet during the day, including many officers. Lewis Gunners relieved tonight by 8th D.L.I.	
	8.7.16		Enemy artillery and Trench Mortars more active but chiefly on L. Trenches. To our Right 3 German Officers seen to look over parapet at our spot. One is described as follows: "About 40, thin grey hair, intelligent. Coloured appearance wearing field grey soft cap with red piping and chin-peak; with 2 badges or cockades.	

Army Form C. 2118.

WAR DIARY
or
INTELLIGENCE SUMMARY.
(Erase heading not required.)

Instructions regarding War Diaries and Intelligence Summaries are contained in F.S. Regs., Part II. and the Staff Manual respectively. Title pages will be prepared in manuscript.

Place	Date	Hour	Summary of Events and Information	Remarks and references to Appendices
	8.7.16		Enemy's trenches show signs of continued activity in repair.	
	9.7.16		Our snipers have almost stopped the enemy's sniping, 16 pts contributing by displacing some of their loopholes during a "strafe" on Orders O. 7. c. 34. (Bois Quarante). The Battalion was relieved tonight by the 8th D.W. and proceed to LA CLYTTE in Divisional Reserve.	
LA CLYTTE	10.7.16 to 15.7.16		The Battalion remained at LA CLYTTE, furnishing working parties every night to carry cables at VIERSTRAAT & for other works.	
	16.7.16		The Battalion proceeded to KEMMEL SHELTERS in Divisional Reserve and continued to find working parties for repairs & new works in the Divisional area. Each day & night thus employing every available man.	
D&E TRENCHES	19.7.16		The Battalion was suddenly called upon to take over the trenches D.5. & 6 & E.1. from the 8th Bn. THE BUFFS (E. KENT REGT) and carried out the relief tonight.	
	20.7.16		The night 19th-20th was uneventful. Machine Gun & front rifle fire persistent and accurate and in early morning a German Sniper into one of our periscopes in the BULL RING. Our trenches have two suitable sniping posts so clearly this annoyance.	
	21.7.16		Machine Gun and Rifle fire again persistent. A patrol under Capt. A.C.R. BLAIR. DSO.	

went out from D.S. and reach the German wire, but they could find no gap. They returned about 1-45 am owing to bright moon-light fearing that it would expose the patrol. Going out a few minutes later to point out a spot where some small repairs to our own wire could be made in a very little time. Capt. BLAIR was hit by a bullet and died two hours later without regaining consciousness. The loss of such a gallant officer is keenly felt throughout the Battalion.

The following letter from Brigadier General CLIFFORD, CMG, D.S.O., Commanding 149th Inf Bde. has since been received by Col. Hedley:-

22.7.16 "Dear Colonel Hedley.- I cannot tell you how distressed I am to hear that "Capt. Blair has been killed. There never was a more gallant officer and I know "what the loss must be to you and your Battn. Please convey to all ranks of "your Battn. my deep sympathy with them in their loss"

Yours very Sincerely.- H.S. Clifford."

A wire in similar terms was also sent by MAJOR-GENL WILKINSON Commanding 50th Division.

WAR DIARY
or
INTELLIGENCE SUMMARY.
(Erase heading not required.)

Army Form C. 2118.

Place	Date	Hour	Summary of Events and Information	Remarks and references to Appendices
	21.7.16		A draft of 150 other ranks joined and Capt. W.F. SPEDDING re-joined the Battalion.	
	22.7.16		Spent actively in digging and reversing German Close Support Line, high manner of earth being thrown up. The day was uneventful. A draft of 130 other ranks joined the Battalion remaining at the Transport Lines to CLYTTE until the Battalion went out on relief.	
	23.7.16		A draft of 89 other ranks joined the Battalion. The Bn. was relieved tonight by the 9th Bn D.L.I. and proceeded to BADAJOZ HUTS, LOCRE in Divisional Reserve. Enemy artillery active on several occasions during the day on D5 Supports. Another minenwerfer thingummy. A minenwerfer shell fell short in the enemy front line trench and the explosion threw up in the air a set of equipment, the bayonet being flung over our line. It afforded no clue as to the occupants of the trenches opposite. Enemy's night sniping considerably less. Our Snipers got 3 hits, and reported that in early morning 4 to 5 trees are visible in prospect opposite through which men have been seen to fire from hip level. After one German had	

Army Form C. 2118.

WAR DIARY
or
INTELLIGENCE SUMMARY.
(Erase heading not required.)

Instructions regarding War Diaries and Intelligence Summaries are contained in F.S. Regs., Part II. and the Staff Manual respectively. Title pages will be prepared in manuscript.

Place	Date	Hour	Summary of Events and Information	Remarks and references to Appendices
			been hit. By our snipers bullet gaps were quickly closed and cavities shown over to disguise the gaps. Enemy continues to work steadily on the new close support trench particularly about N.30.c.6.0. The change in enemy attitude in regard to M.G. & Rifle fire seems to point to a relief having taken place and the artillery fire though following our previous practice seems more of the nature of registration.	
LOCRE	24.7.16		The Companies were kept busy apportioning to platoons the kits of men allotted to each and completing their recepts and inspecting kits. All the men just returned from the trenches attended at DRANOUTRE for baths & change of clothing.	
	25.7.16		A large Working Party of 500 other ranks under the command of Major Sowlsby and 17 other officers were called upon for the task of carrying out at the front line trenches in the Divisional Area, all the gas cylinders which had been from time to time placed in position there. The long march to and from the trenches and the heavy work – each cylinder requiring at least two	

Army Form C. 2118.

WAR DIARY
or
INTELLIGENCE SUMMARY.
(Erase heading not required.)

Instructions regarding War Diaries and Intelligence Summaries are contained in F. S. Regs., Part II. and the Staff Manual respectively. Title pages will be prepared in manuscript.

Place	Date	Hour	Summary of Events and Information	Remarks and references to Appendices
			own to carry it with a third hand to carry the rifles of the âme so occupied. Although fatigued, the men did not return to Camp until 5 a.m. having set out at 7 p.m. The work was evidently very willingly & satisfactorily carried out. A letter of appreciation of the importance and danger of the work & of the satisfactory way in which it was done being received from Captain W. Anderson, Brigade Major, 149th Infantry Brigade.	Appendix
	25/7/16		Lewis Gunners relieved the 9th D.L.I. in the Trenches E.1., E.2, F.2, F.4, & F.5. a night in advance of the rest of the Battalion.	
TRENCHES. E.1, E.2, F.2, F.4, F.5. and Supports	26/7/16		The Battalion moved into the line in the relief of the 9th D.L.I. the Brigade front having been re-apportioned owing to the recently augmented strength of our Bn. "C" Company (Capt. D. McGlass) took over trenches E.1. (including "Bull Ring") E.2. and part of F.2. "D" Company (Capt.) A.B. Cowburn) took over trenches F.2, part, F.4. F.5. The Battalion front extending from N.30. c.5.0. to N.29.J. 9-6. Sheet 28. "A" Company (Capt. J.N. Robinson) took over support points No. 8, 9, 10 and PICCADILLY Keeps. "B" Company (Capt. S. Rigg) finding the garrisons of FORTS EDWARD, VICTORIA & REGINA	

T. M34. Wt. W708–776. 500000. 4/15. Sir J. C. & S.

WAR DIARY
or
INTELLIGENCE SUMMARY.
(Erase heading not required.)

Army Form C. 2118.

Place	Date	Hour	Summary of Events and Information	Remarks and references to Appendices
	27/7/16		and the REGENT St. Dugouts in Bn. Reserve. During the night enemy put up a considerable number of flares and shot from snipers and short rifles were frequent and accurate in many places ripping the sandbags of our parapets. Artillery was active for a few minutes only. A lucky shot from the enemy's point of view hitting a dugout in support line causing us four casualties amongst the bombers who were resting there. A sharp duel between minenwerfers and trench mortars developed about 4 pm in the "G" Trenches on our immediate left but did not touch our area.	
	28/7/16		Machine Gun and fixed rifle fire active during the night until 2.30. Remained again about 3.0 am. Probably a relief took place in enemy trenches opposite at this time. Artillery & T.M. on enemy side were quiet. Our fires spasmodically in short bursts. Enemy snipers quiet during day. Ours got two hits. Patrols under Lt. O. J. FEETHAM & Lt. J. N. FRANKS were out in No Mans Land for considerable	

WAR DIARY
or
INTELLIGENCE SUMMARY.

Army Form C. 2118.

Place	Date	Hour	Summary of Events and Information	Remarks and references to Appendices
	29/7/16		periods, but found no sign of enemy's patrol. 2/Lt FEETHAM's patrol brought in a set of British Web Equipment across which they stumbled. At 3.10 p.m. six enemy bombs were thrown over the parapet. Two enemy aeroplanes were observed but they were on each occasion chased back by our machines which showed great activity throughout the afternoon. Our Artillery fired a good number of rounds on front line and support trenches opposite the Bull RING. The night was similar to the previous in M.G.s and Rifle action in the early hours. A patrol under 2/Lt JEH COOMBES was out for 1½ hours but had nothing to report of enemy activity.	
	30/7/16		Enemy Artillery and T.M. awoke twice during the day and placed some heavy shells in our area, without doing any damage. We retaliated with rifle grenades, Stokes T.M. and 18 pdrs. which must have been equally effective. Patrol under 2/Lt. E.W. FAGAN worked towards German trench in front of F.5 and found	

WAR DIARY
or
INTELLIGENCE SUMMARY.
(Erase heading not required.)

Army Form C. 2118.

Place	Date	Hour	Summary of Events and Information	Remarks and references to Appendices
			signs of enemy activity. Listening Posts reported hearing two blasts of a whistle (shrill blastfall) from the enemy trench. They also heard a party some 30 distance away and L.G. fired on the suspected locality. Enemy snipers pierced one of our loop-hole plates with an armour piercing bullet having apparently fired some of this ammunition especially after exchanging three shots with one of our snipers. Fortunately no one was behind the plate at the time. Six of our aeroplanes crossed the German lines and it was noticed that three enemy Observation Balloons were immediately lowered. As soon as our planes returned up the Balloons rose again.	
	31-7-16		Artillery quiet. Rifle fire and M. Guns active during the night from 8 p.m. having commenced earlier than usual probably in retaliation for the fire of one of our machine guns in support and of a rifle battery which was using rifle in his parapet. One of our Nieuport Planes apparently took the enemy by surprise by flying low over the SPANBROEKMOLEN Salient. Anti-Aircraft Guns were	

silent but eventually snipers and M.G. fired at him & he returned. Much aircraft activity during afternoon and day very favourable for observation. Enemy used a heavier shell on our containing higher explosive than usual against our planes which however all returned safe so far as could be seen. In the night of 30th - 31st Lieut J.N. FRANKS took out a patrol and found signs in the form of recent occupation. of certain spots. A track lead from there to the German lines and the patrol followed it up until they came to that place which afforded no cover. Nothing was seen of any German Patrol. A little sniping activity. Wall of sandbagged bays of dugouts noticeable in German lines in a few places. Little or nothing seems to have been done on the work in enemy close support lines where recently high mounds of earth have been thrown up.

[signature]
L.Col. 5th Border Regt.

The following letter has been received :-

151st Infantry Brigade.

I shall be glad if the enclosed may be forwarded to the 5th Border Regt - who took part in this work:

"The Brigade Commander wishes to express his appreciation to all concerned for the very successful manner in which the special work has been carried out during the last two nights.

This work, which entails a great deal of risk and requires very careful organisation, had to be carried out at short notice in an area which was very largely new to the troops, and the complete success of the operations is a high tribute to the efficient arrangements made by the Battalions concerned and by the special Company, R.E., and to the work of the officers and men of the carrying parties.

Please cause this to be communicated to all concerned."

(Sd) Wm. Andersen, Captain,
27/7/16.   Brigade Major, 149th Infantry Brigade.

Army Form C. 2118.

WAR DIARY
or
INTELLIGENCE SUMMARY

(Erase heading not required.)

War Diary

1/5th Battⁿ The Border Reg⁺.

August 1916

Volume No. X

Vol XI

Army Form C. 2118.

WAR DIARY
or
INTELLIGENCE SUMMARY

(Erase heading not required.)

Instructions regarding War Diaries and Intelligence Summaries are contained in F. S. Regs., Part II. and the Staff Manual respectively. Title Pages will be prepared in manuscript.

Place	Date	Hour	Summary of Events and Information	Remarks and references to Appendices
	1-8-16		The night was normal as to M.G. and Rifle fire. Today very quiet. Enemy snipers did not trouble us and ours had few targets. But managed to annoy the sentries and snipers by breaking periscopes and chipping loop-hole plates, the hole in one being enlarged through the edges being chipped by bullets. A rifle battery worried the enemy by firing for some hours as to this parapet. 2/Lt. COOMBES with 10 men went out on patrol during the night 31st/1st to the spot where shots had been directed the previous night and lay in wait for 2 hours without seeing anything of enemy patrols. This was the fifth consecutive patrol that has seen no movement in front of the enemy trench. One of our officers and a N.C.O. caught an enemy working party on the mounds opposite the BULL RING and succeeded for fact, causing the work to cease. A bursting Rifle Grenade fire was sent in return and an explosion of some stride. The day was also hazy for minute observation. The Battalion was relieved by the 9th Bn. Suffolk L.I. in Trenches E.T.F. and Support	
AIRCRAFT FARM. KEMMEL	1-8-16 to 6-8-16		Points and moved to Bde. Reserve at AIRCRAFT FARM, KEMMEL, where everyone was pleased again to the smell canvas or in bivouacs, the weather being graciously fine. Working Parties were found every night for work in C.T.'s or at dugouts, behind the line recently left.	

Army Form C. 2118.

WAR DIARY
or
INTELLIGENCE SUMMARY

(Erase heading not required.)

Instructions regarding War Diaries and Intelligence Summaries are contained in F.S. Regs., Part II. and the Staff Manual respectively. Title Pages will be prepared in manuscript.

Place	Date	Hour	Summary of Events and Information	Remarks and references to Appendices
BOESCHEPE.	6-8-16 to 10-8-16		On the night of the 6th/7th about 11-30pm the Bn. moved to BOESCHEPE, (the same area in which it had been training during the rest in April & May) handing over to the 8th Bn. NORTH STAFFORDSHIRE REGIMENT, 19th Division as part of the Divisional Relief. The four days spent here were mainly spent in preparation for the move shortly to take place and in the very early morning of the 11th August the Battalion marched to	
DIVISIONAL MOVE. Entrained at GODEWAERSVELDE.	11-8-16		GODEWAERSVELDE, and entrained for the South, A Company acting as the baggage party. The entrainment was carried out satisfactorily and without undue trouble or delay, the journey being commenced shortly to scheduled time 5.31 am.	
	11-8-16		Arrived at CANDAS (PICARDY) about 11 am, and detrained and marched to BEAUMETZ in easy stages, a half being made for dinner as soon as the village of CANDAS was left behind. BEAUMETZ was reached by 5 p.m. and became our home until the 15th August. Route marches twice a day in fighting, or full marching order were carried out in order to harden us for the moves before us.	
VIGNACOURT	15-8-16		The Divisional move was continued by Bde. marches. This Battalion moving first at 4-15 am in the column to VIGNACOURT.	
	16-8-16		MAJOR A.D. SOURSBY appointed Town-major of BEHENCOURT and FRECHENCOURT, and accompanied the Battalion as far as VILLERS BOCAGE on the way to take up this	

Army Form C. 2118.

WAR DIARY
or
INTELLIGENCE SUMMARY

(Erase heading not required.)

Instructions regarding War Diaries and Intelligence Summaries are contained in F.S. Regs., Part II. and the Staff Manual respectively. Title Pages will be prepared in manuscript.

Place	Date	Hour	Summary of Events and Information	Remarks and references to Appendices
	16.8.16		appointment. CAPTAIN A.B. COWBURN appointed 2nd in Command and CAPTAIN W.F. SPEDDING assuming command of "D" Company at VIGNACOURT.	
RAINNEVILLE	16.8.16		The march was continued at 10.0 a.m. in the same manner with this Battalion at the rear of the column, via FRESSENNES & VILLARS BOCAGE to RAINNEVILLE.	
BAIZIEUX WOOD	17.8.16		March continued by the way of MONTIGNY & BEHENCOURT to BAIZIEUX WOOD, which was reached by midday. The afternoon was spent in erecting tents or bivouacs, and the rain which fell at night taught everyone a lesson in constructing a bivouac which would keep out the wet.	
	18.8.16		A Course of instruction in sharpshooting was organised by the III Corps to which 2/Lt. FAGAN and 2 of D Company Snipers were sent.	
	19.8.16		Lt: 386 L/Sgt. W.H. LEE (Sniper) was called upon to act as an instructor at the 50th Divisional Sniping School at BEHENCOURT and remained there on the 19th. 16 Snipers from this Battalion were put through this Course.	
	20.8.16		Other Courses of instruction to which men were sent included (a) Lewis Gun Course, (b) Contact Patrol Buzzer Course. (R.F.C.). The Battalion furnished a working party of one Officer and 60 other ranks to report at MERICOURT, No. 6. R.E. Park at 5 p.m. Buses being provided to convey them to and fro.	

Army Form C. 2118.

WAR DIARY
or
INTELLIGENCE SUMMARY
(Erase heading not required.)

Instructions regarding War Diaries and Intelligence Summaries are contained in F. S. Regs., Part II. and the Staff Manual respectively. Title Pages will be prepared in manuscript.

Place	Date	Hour	Summary of Events and Information	Remarks and references to Appendices
	28.8.16		Divisional Parade ordered for this day cancelled owing to inclement weather. The two representatives of this Battalion who were, as this parade to have the ribbons of the D.C.M. pinned on their breasts by the Corps Commander Lt General Sir W.P. PURTENEY, K.C.B, D.S.O. attended at the 149th Inf. Bde. H.Q. at HENENCOURT later in the day where the ceremony was performed. They were:- 271 Acting Coy. Sgt. Major T. AITKEN to whom it was awarded on 2.6.16 for conspicuous gallantry and devotion to duty in organising and personally superintending the wiring parties of his Company for the last 10 months. + 1490 Sgt. (Actg. A/Sgt.) G.S. MARTIN to whom with Sgt. PAGAN it was given for conspicuous gallantry in laying wire between Coy. & Bn. H.Q. during the heavy bombardment on 19-1-16, involving taking wires across the open.	
	29.8.16		The 151st Brigade practice of an attack arranged for today was also postponed on account of the heavy rain and the men suffered much from the same cause, lying as they were in bivouacs. Arrangements were made this day to billet part of the Battalion in the village of BAIZIEUX, and on the	
	30.8.16		'B' & 'D' Coy. and the Lewis Gunners moved into these billets and were thereafter sorely their clothes. The men of the Battalion suffered from a considerable amount of sickness due probably to the difficulty of getting their clothes dried.	

Army Form C. 2118.

WAR DIARY
or
INTELLIGENCE SUMMARY

(Erase heading not required.)

Instructions regarding War Diaries and Intelligence Summaries are contained in F.S. Regs., Part II. and the Staff Manual respectively. Title Pages will be prepared in manuscript.

Place	Date	Hour	Summary of Events and Information	Remarks and references to Appendices
	31.8.16		During the period the Brigade has been encamped in BAIZIEUX WOOD. There has been frequent opportunities for much needed Range Practice and in anticipation of sharing in conditions of fighting of a different character than experienced up to date attention has been given specially to "The Attack" both in trenches and in the open. Unfortunately rain has interfered with our programme of training.	

151st. INFANTRY BRIGADE
50th. DIVISION

5th. BORDER REGT.

151st. INFANTRY BRIGADE

SEPTEMBER 1916.

Army Form C. 2118.

WAR DIARY
~~INTELLIGENCE SUMMARY~~
(Erase heading not required.)

15/350
15/10
Vol 12

5" Bn. The Border Regt.

September, 1916.

Volume N° 12

Army Form C. 2118.

WAR DIARY
or
INTELLIGENCE SUMMARY

(Erase heading not required.)

Instructions regarding War Diaries and Intelligence Summaries are contained in F.S. Regs., Part II. and the Staff Manual respectively. Title Pages will be prepared in manuscript.

Place	Date	Hour	Summary of Events and Information	Remarks and references to Appendices
BAIZIEUX WOOD.	1-9-16 to 10-9-16		Battalion bivouaced in BAIZIEUX WOOD and part in BAIZIEUX VILLAGE and was engaged in training in musketry and Battalion, Brigade and Divisional practices.	
	10-9-16		The Battalion moved by route march to BECOURT WOOD via MILLECOURT – ALBERT and encamped in bivouacs.	
	11-9-16 to 12-9-16		Two large working parties were provided in the early morning and afternoon for the purpose of burying cable near RAILWAY COPSE X.28.b.3.0. Sheet 57d.	
	14-9-16		Battalion march at dusk to SHELTER WOOD. X.28.a.5.10. Sheet 57d	
	15-9-16 to 16-9-16		At 6-20 a.m. Battalion moved forward to QUADRANGLE TRENCH about X.22.d.5.4. About 12 noon the Battalion moved to trenches S.W. corner of MAMETZ WOOD. About 6.30 p.m. Battalion was ordered to move up and attack and capture with the rest of the 151st Infantry Brigade, the second and third objectives, namely; STAR FISH LINE and PRUE TRENCH about M.33.b. and M.34.a. Sheet 57c S.W. Rations again before passing the Brigade Headquarters at the QUARRIES where guides were provided. The guides however, in moving forward lost their direction and the Battalion did not reach the assembly trench, about S.3.a.7.c central	

WAR DIARY
or
INTELLIGENCE SUMMARY

Army Form C. 2118.

Place	Date	Hour	Summary of Events and Information	Remarks and references to Appendices
	15.9.16 to 16.9.16		until about half-an-hour after the time laid down. About 11 p.m. the Battalion was ordered to its objective and got in touch with the 6th and 9th D.L.I. some of whom had already gone. Owing to the darkness and general state of the ground the Battalion did not reach its objective but moved forward about 6 to 700 yards and dug themselves in in THE BOW C.T. owing to the advancing daylight. Some H.Q. details had been ordered to move forward in support of the rest of the Battalion and they eventually got in touch with part of 'B' Company and part of the 6th D.L.I. getting up almost to the STAR FISH LINE on the left of THE BOW but were driven back by M.G. fire, joining up with the rest of the Battalion and digging in between THE BOW and CRESENT ALLEY. During these operations the Battalion lost in killed:- Lieut. G.H. DAWES V/Adjutant, 2/Lieut. R.P. BAXTER, wounded Capt. W.F. SPEDDING, 2/Lieuts. J.E.H. COOMBES, F.J. LAIN and E.J. PURSGLOVE and about 100 other ranks killed and wounded.	
	17.9.16		Battalion remain in its former position about THE BOW and improved the trenches. Capt. M.R. INGLIS (R.A.M.C.) was killed whilst attending the wounded in the field during the night.	

WAR DIARY or INTELLIGENCE SUMMARY

Army Form C. 2118.

Place	Date	Hour	Summary of Events and Information	Remarks and references to Appendices
	17.9.16		On the night of the 17th/18th "A" Company was withdrawn to the HOOK TRENCH.	
	18.9.16		The Battalion was ordered in conjunction with the rest of Brigade to attack STAR FISH LINE at 5.50 a.m. At the appointed hour Companies in the front line left the trenches for the attack but they did not reach the objective owing to the sodden condition of the ground and again heavy M.G. fire. Capt. D.W. GLASS and 2/Lieut. A. FEETHAM were killed. Lieut. H.P. SMITH was wounded and about 60 other ranks killed and wounded. 2/Lieut. S. HALL was shell shocked and was sent to hospital.	
	19.9.16		The Companies in about the BOW were relieved by the 8th D.L.I and withdrew to SWANSEA TRENCH that night. "A" Company moved from the HOOK TRENCH and occupied strong post at the N.W. corner of HIGH WOOD in S.3.b. and came under the orders of the 8th D.L.I.	
	20.9.16		The Battalion was relieved in the SWANSEA TRENCH and Strong Post by the 4th N.F. 149th Inf. Brigade and moved to trenches S.W. corner of MAMETZ WOOD. The following letter was received from the B.G.C. 151st Inf. Brigade:- "I have been asked by the Divisional Commander to convey his warm thanks to the four Battalions of the 151st Infantry Brigade for the	

WAR DIARY
or
INTELLIGENCE SUMMARY

Army Form C. 2118.

Place	Date	Hour	Summary of Events and Information	Remarks and references to Appendices
			whole Leaders efforts they have made during the arduous operations of the last few days and for the success which they have achieved. It would have liked very much to have come round to see Battalion Commanders personally had the time or opportunity to do so at present. For myself, I should like to add that I am full of admiration for the soldierly spirit displayed by all ranks of the four Battalions in the attack and their endurance under very considerable hardships, privation and exertion lasting nearly a week. (Sd) N.J.G. Cameron, Brigadier General Commanding 151st Infantry Brigade. 20th September, 1916.	
	23.9.16		Working Party was provided for repairing roads at BAZENTIN LE PETIT	
	24.9.16		Battalion moved forward at 1 pm. and relieved 5th Bn. N.F., 149th Brigade in SWANSEA TRENCH and CLARKS TRENCH.	
	25.9.16	9.15 pm	a working party of about 280 moved forward and dug an assembly trench from about M.28.d.1.7½ to M.28.b.5.2 (Sheet 57c SW.) and C.T. M.28.d.1.7½ to M.28.b.5.2 — M.28.b.10.0 — M.28.b.0.3. (Sheet 57c SW.) withdrawing to its former position at 3.45 a.m.	

WAR DIARY
or
INTELLIGENCE SUMMARY

(Erase heading not required.)

Army Form C. 2118.

Place	Date	Hour	Summary of Events and Information	Remarks and references to Appendices
	26.9.16		During the night a covering party under 2/Lieut. H. PRIDE captured a prisoner of the 23rd Infantry Regiment. Battalion was ordered to Stand to in its trenches at 11 p.m. and support if necessary an attack to be made by the 150th Bde.	
	27.9.16		At 12.15 am Battalion was ordered to "Stand Down" and remain ready to move at a quarter of an hour's notice. About 3 am 'A' & 'B' Companies were ordered to move forward and occupy the BOAST TRENCH, 'C' Company TYNE STREET and D Company HOOK TRENCH. Two Companies B+C were placed at the disposal of the 5th Battalion Yorkshire Regiment. The Battalion was ordered to relieve the 5th Bn. Yorkshire Regiment in PRUE TRENCH, STAR FISH LINE and CRESENT ALLEY. During the night 'B' & 'C' Companies moved forward to occupy trench vacated temporarily by 8th D.L.I. and eventually withdrew to their former positions on the morning of the 29.9th.	
	29.9.16		In the evening "A" Company had to be withdrawn and was ordered back to an isolation camp near FRICOURT on account of outbreak of dysentery. About 7.30 p.m. "B" "C" & "D" Companies were ordered to move up to reinforce	

Army Form C. 2118.

WAR DIARY
or
INTELLIGENCE SUMMARY
(Erase heading not required.)

Instructions regarding War Diaries and Intelligence Summaries are contained in F. S. Regs., Part II. and the Staff Manual respectively. Title Pages will be prepared in manuscript.

Place	Date	Hour	Summary of Events and Information	Remarks and references to Appendices
	29.9.16		The 8th D.L.I. who were engaged in a Bombing Attack on their immediate front about M.22.a.7&.0. to M.22.a.2.&. "B" Company occupied NORTH DURHAM STREET and CRESENT ALLEY.	
	30.9.16		In the early morning "C"+"D" Companies moved up into 26th AVENUE relieving 8th D.L.I. Companies there and in SPENCE STREET.	

A.L. Jones
2/Lt
4 Aug
3rd Border Reg.

151/50

151st Infantry Brigade.

       Herewith volumn 11 and particulars of Officers for War Diary of 5TH BATTALION, THE BORDER REGIMENT, please.

                                                          Lieut. & Adjutant,

1 /11/16.   for O.C. 5th Battalion, The Border Regiment.

WAR DIARY
or
INTELLIGENCE SUMMARY.
(Erase heading not required.)

Army Form C. 2118.

Hour, Date, Place	Summary of Events and Information	Remarks and references to Appendices
1.10.16	Battalion was ordered to attack and capture the first and support lines of trenches in the FLERS LINE about M.22.a.7½.0. to M.22.a.2.½. and support line M.22.a.7½.8½ to M.29.a.2.3. The attack to be made in four waves by three companies each on a platoon front. The first and second waves comprised of 8th Border Regiment, third and fourth wave 8½Bn. D.L.I. The objective for the first and third wave was the German Support line and objective for second and fourth wave was the German first line. The attack was timed to commence at 3.15 p.m. (ZERO) after prolonged artillery bombardment. When the bombardment lifted at the time stated the first wave left the assembly trench (North Durham Street) and followed close up to the barrage line, followed	

Army Form C. 2118.

WAR DIARY
or
INTELLIGENCE SUMMARY.
(Erase heading not required.)

Instructions regarding War Diaries and Intelligence Summaries are contained in F.S. Regs., Part II. and the Staff Manual respectively. Title pages will be prepared in manuscript.

Hour, Date, Place	Summary of Events and Information	Remarks and references to Appendices
1-10-16	by the other three waves at intervals of 50 yards. The two lines were captured before the enemy realized that we were in possession. A very small number only of the Battalion on our right reached the first objective the result being that the Composite Battalion of 5th Border Regt. & 8th Bn. R.I. had a very strenuous and responsible time in clearing their right flank and forming blocks thereto. An enemy machine gun was captured in the first objective just as it was beginning to cause trouble. The position was held and consolidated until	
2.10.16	the following night Oct. 2nd when we were relieved by the 4th Bn. N.F. and withdrew to SWANSEA TRENCH. Owing to the congestion in the Communication Trenches the relief was not completed until about 5 AM and the Battalion reached its destination about 7 AM.	

Army Form C. 2118.

WAR DIARY
or
INTELLIGENCE SUMMARY.
(Erase heading not required.)

Instructions regarding War Diaries and Intelligence Summaries are contained in F.S. Regs., Part II. and the Staff Manual respectively. Title pages will be prepared in manuscript.

Hour, Date, Place	Summary of Events and Information	Remarks and references to Appendices
3.10.16	At 12 noon the Battalion marched to BECOURT WOOD and bivouaced there for the night.	
4.10.16	At 11 a.m. the Battalion marched to midnest at HENENCOURT WOOD having had a meal on the way between ALBERT and MILLENCOURT and we reached our destination about 4 p.m.	
5.10.16 & 6.10.16	The Battalion was bathed and clothed and time was spent in generally cleaning up. The following letter was published by the G.O.C. 50th Division. "Nobody could be prouder than I am of commanding such troops as you of the 50th Division. Within a few days of landing in this country you made a name for yourselves at the Second Battle of YPRES. Since that battle you have gained a great reputation on account of your magnificent defence of a portion of the YPRES Salient during the	

Army Form C. 2118.

WAR DIARY
or
INTELLIGENCE SUMMARY.
(Erase heading not required.)

Instructions regarding War Diaries and Intelligence Summaries are contained in F. S. Regs., Part II. and the Staff Manual respectively. Title pages will be prepared in manuscript.

Hour, Date, Place	Summary of Events and Information	Remarks and references to Appendices
	worst months of the year. From September the 15th to October 3rd you have had another chance of showing your qualities in attack and it is not too much to say that no Division in the British Army has, or could have, done better. You have advanced nearly two miles and have taken seven lines of German trenches. Your gallantry and determination in every occasion since you joined in the Battle of the Somme has been worthy of the highest traditions of the British Army. I deplore with you the loss of many of our comrade friends and comrades. I thank you all for the excellent and cheerful way in which you have undertaken every task put to you. (Sgd) P. S. Wilkinson, Major General Commanding 50th (Northumbrian) Div.	

Forms/C. 2418/10

Army Form C. 2118.

WAR DIARY
or
INTELLIGENCE SUMMARY.
(Erase heading not required.)

Instructions regarding War Diaries and Intelligence Summaries are contained in F. S. Regs., Part II. and the Staff Manual respectively. Title pages will be prepared in manuscript.

Hour, Date, Place	Summary of Events and Information	Remarks and references to Appendices
6-10-16 to 16-10-16	Brigade and Divisional training during this period. Large working parties were also supplied by the Battalion. The following was received from 3rd Corps through the usual channels:- "Report on Operation on the 1st Oct as seen from the air" "At 3.15 p.m. the heavy bombardment changed into a most magnificent barrage. The timing of this was extremely good. Guns opened simultaneously and the effect was that of many machine Guns opening fire on the same order. As seen from the air the barrage appeared to be a most perfect wall of fire in which it was inconceivable that anything could live. The first troops do extend from the forming up places appeared to be the 50th Division who were seen to spread out from the Tap heads and forming up trenches and advance close up under the barrage.	

Army Form C. 2118.

WAR DIARY
or
INTELLIGENCE SUMMARY.
(Erase heading not required.)

Instructions regarding War Diaries and Intelligence Summaries are contained in F.S. Regs., Part II. and the Staff Manual respectively. Title pages will be prepared in manuscript.

Hour, Date, Place	Summary of Events and Information	Remarks and references to Appendices
	apparently some 50 yards away from it. They appeared to capture their objective very rapidly and with practically no losses while crossing the open. The 23rd Division I did not see so much of owing to their being at the moment of Zero at the tail end of the machine. The 47th Division took more looking for than the 50th and it was my impression at the time that they were having some difficulty in getting into formation for attack from their forming up places, with the result that they appeared to be very late and to be some distance behind the barrage when it lifted off the German Front line at EAUCOURT L'ABBAYE and immediately do the west of it. It was plain that here there was a good chance of failure and this actually came about, for the men	

Forms/C. 2118/10

WAR DIARY
or
INTELLIGENCE SUMMARY.
(Erase heading not required.)

Army Form C. 2118.

Instructions regarding War Diaries and Intelligence Summaries are contained in F.S. Regs., Part II. and the Staff Manual respectively. Title pages will be prepared in manuscript.

Hour, Date, Place	Summary of Events and Information	Remarks and references to Appendices
	had hardly advanced a couple of hundred yards apparently, when they were seen to fall and take cover among shell holes, being presumably held up by Machine Gun and rifle fire. It was not possible to verify this owing to the extraordinary noise of the bursting shells of our barrage. The tanks were obviously days far behind, owing to lack of covered approaches, to be able to take part in the original attack, but they were seen later advancing in leisurely pace of the EAUCOURT L'ABBAYE — FLERS Line, continuously in action and doing splendid work. They did not seem to be a target of much enemy shell fire. The enemy barrage appeared to open late, quite five minutes after the commencement of our own barrage, and when it came it bore no resemblance	

WAR DIARY
or
INTELLIGENCE SUMMARY.
(Erase heading not required.)

Army Form C. 2118.

Instructions regarding War Diaries and Intelligence Summaries are contained in F. S. Regs., Part II. and the Staff Manual respectively. Title pages will be prepared in manuscript.

Hour, Date, Place	Summary of Events and Information	Remarks and references to Appendices
	of the wall of fire which we were putting up. I should have described it as a heavy shelling of an area some 3 to 400 yds. in depth from our original jumping off places. Some large shells were falling in DESIREMONT FARM but these again were too late to catch the first line of attack, although they must have caused some losses to the supports. 30 minutes after zero the first English patrols were seen entering LE SARS. They appeared to be meeting with little or no opposition. And at this time no German shells were falling in the village. Our own shells were falling in the Northern half. To sum up: The most startling feature of the operations as viewed from the air was the extraordinary volume of fire of our barrage	

WAR DIARY
or
INTELLIGENCE SUMMARY.
(Erase heading not required.)

Army Form C. 2118.

Hour, Date, Place	Summary of Events and Information	Remarks and references to Appendices
	and the straight line kept by it.	
	(2) The apparent ease with which the attack succeeded where troops were enabled to go forward close under it.	
	(3) The promiscuous character and comparative lack of volume of enemy's counter-barrage.	
	(sgd) J. Charnier, Major Commanding 34th Squadron, R.F.C. Extract from London Gazette dated 11.10.16 :-	
8th October 1916.	1599 2/Sgt Agnew J.A. 2090 L/Sgt Bigrigg J. 2087 Cpt Clemead R. 947 " Cole J. 3103 Pte Fell Jas. 1299 " James J. 1417 " Charis J. 2134 " Linton W. 1425 " Tipper W. } Awarded the MILITARY MEDAL	
17.10.16	The Battalion moved to MAMETZ WOOD leaving HENENCOURT WOOD at 10 a.m. and marching via	

Army Form C. 2118.

WAR DIARY
or
INTELLIGENCE SUMMARY.
(Erase heading not required.)

5th Border Regt

Hour, Date, Place	Summary of Events and Information	Remarks and references to Appendices
	MILLENCOURT and ALBERT having dinner on the way about 12.30 p.m. All available men were employed repairing roads from 5 A.m to 2.30 p.m. daily. The Transport and Quartermasters Store remained at HENENCOURT WOOD during this period.	769.- 81-
22.10.16	The Battalion moved back to HENENCOURT WOOD. A draft of 46 other ranks joined Battalion to day. Extract from 50th Division Routine Orders dated 21.10.16 :- The Corps Commander has awarded the following decoration to the undermentioned men :- 2426 Pte Teilor W. 2955 " Teilor J.T. 2931 " Suttle J.K. } MILITARY MEDAL. 1543 " Pearson J. 2891 " Banks H.W.B.	
23.10.16	The Battalion moved from HENENCOURT WOOD to a place near BECOURT, and pitched tents	

Army Form C. 2118.

WAR DIARY
or
INTELLIGENCE SUMMARY.
(Erase heading not required.)

Instructions regarding War Diaries and Intelligence Summaries are contained in F.S. Regs., Part II. and the Staff Manual respectively. Title pages will be prepared in manuscript.

Hour, Date, Place	Summary of Events and Information	Remarks and references to Appendices
25.10.16	The Battalion moved to MAMETZ WOOD and relieved the 12th Bn. Royal Scots, leaving BECOURT about 9.15 a.m.	
26.10.16	A working party of 2 Officers, 5 N.C.O.s and 100 men was supplied parading at S.3.a.4.8. at 9 a.m. for work on the tramways.	
27.10.16 to 31.10.16	The Battalion supplied large carrying and working parties daily for road making. The Battalion Camp was moved to fresh ground. Officers reconnoitring various routes to front line and supports.	

770-
EB

J Mackie Lt Adjt
for O.C. 5th The Border Rgt.

5TH BATTALION THE BORDER REGIMENT

Particulars of Officers.

Officers who came to France 25/10/14.

Lt.Col. T.A. Milburn	Invalided to England 25/7/15.
Major A.C. Scoular	Invalided to England 23/3/15.
Major A.D. Soulsby	T/Lt.Col. 23/3/15. T/Major 11/11/15. To 36th Labour Bn. 10/9/16.
Captain A.F. Broadley-Smith	T/Major 13/4/15. Killed in action 16/6/15.
Captain H.J. Bewley	T/Major 17/6/15. To England 22/2/16.
Captain R.C.R. Blair, D.S.O.	To England (W.O. Special leave) 21/10/15. Rejoined Bn. 2/2/16. To England (W.O. Special leave) 20/4/16. Rejoined Bn. 24/6/16. Killed in action 21/7/16.
Captain S. Rigg	To England 15/9/15. Rejoined Bn. 25/4/16. Wounded 26/9/16. To England 30/9/16.
Captain W.F. Spedding	To England 3/6/15. Rejoined Bn. 9/8/15. To England 7/1/16. Rejoined Bn. 23/7/16. Wounded 1/9/16.
Captain H.R. Potts	To England 26/12/15.
Captain A.B. Cowburn	To Cadet School, England 13/9/16.
Captain E.A. Iredale	
Lieut. H.C. Webb	T/Captain 18/4/16. To England 26/5/16. Rejoined Bn. 7/7/15. To Stokes Gun Coy. 27/6/16. Killed in action 16/9/16.
Lieut. J.W. Robinson	T/Captain 13/6/15. To England 29/6/15. Rejoined Bn. 7/10/15.
Lieut. W. Adair	To England 12/3/16.
Lieut. W.S. Sewell	To England 20/5/15. Rejoined Bn. 7/10/15. To England 22/5/16.
Lieut. R.J. Rice	T/Captain 16/6/15. Wounded 3/7/15. To England 2 2/8/15.
Lieut. F.B. Spedding	To England 15/3/15. Rejoined Bn. 25/4/15. To England 9/7/16.
Lieut. C.N. Jenkins	To Base duty and struck off strength 29/12/15.
Lieut. F.P. Longmire	To England 19/5/15. Rejoined Bn. 25/4/16. To England 2/8/16.

(2)

Officers who came to France 25/10/14 continued.

2/Lieut. C. Graham	T/Lieut. 18/4/15. Killed in action 27/5/15.
2/Lieut. G. G. Askew	T/Lieut. 18/4/16. Wounded 6/7/15. To England 13/7/15. Rejoined Bn. 25/4/16. To Base duty and struck off strength 16/10/16.
2/Lieut. J. N. Franks	T/Lieut. 20/5/16. To England 29/8/15. Rejoined Bn. 1/1/16. Lieut. 4/6/16. Wounded 1/10/16. To England 6/10/16.
2/Lieut. H. P. Smith	T/Lieut. 19/4/15. Lieut. 24/6/16. Wounded 24/5/15. To England 27/5/15. Rejoined Bn. 25/4/16. Wounded 18/9/16. To England 21/9/16.
2/Lieut. J. B. McGhie	T/Lieut. 17/1/16. To England 30/4/15. Rejoined Bn. 19/12/15. To Base duty 5/8/16.
2/Lieut. I. H. M. Humphreys	Wounded 12/6/15. To England 27/6/15.
2/Lieut. P. W. Maclagan	T/Lieut. 27/5/15. Killed in action 16/4/16.
Major & Q.M.G. Pecker	To England 13/1/16.
Captain & Adj. T.W. MacDonald	To England 29/6/15.
Chaplain & Hon. Lt-Col. Campbell	To England 27/12/14.
Lieut. W. Marley Cass, (RAMC attd)	To England 29/2/15.

Joined Bn. 17/12/14.

2/Lieut. J.W. Adair	Wounded 17/5/15. To England 27/5/15.

Joined Bn. 9/1/15.

2/Lieut. W.F.D. de la Touche	Wounded 24/5/15. To England 21/7/15.

Joined Bn. 12/7/15.

2/Lieut. W.P. Bennett	T/Lieut. 18/7/15. Attd. 151/1 T.M.Bty. Wounded 21/4/15. To England 4/5/16.
2/Lieut. H. Bennett	To England 15/8/15.
2/Lieut. H.E. Wood	T/Lieut. 6/8/15. To 151st M.G.Coy. seconded 6/2/16.
2/Lieut. P.B.C. Holdsworth	T/Lieut. 30/11/15. Wounded 14/7/15. To England 23/7/15. Rejoined Bn. 29/8/16. Wounded 1/10/16. To England 4/10/16.
2/Lieut. A.S. Wilson	T/Lieut 7/2/16. Wounded 25/9/15. To England 25/9/15. Rejoined Bn. 31/1/16 Seconded for duty with T.M.Bty. 16/9/16.

(3)

Joined Bn. 12/7/15.

2/Lieut. C.K. Montgomery — To England 5/12/15.

2/Lieut. D.W. Glass — A/Adjutant 29/7/15. To Duty 12/2/16. T/Captain 3/4/16. Killed in action 13/9/16.

2/Lieut. J.M. Main — Seconded for duty with 182nd Tunn. Coy. R.E. 2/10/15.

2/Lieut. R.B. Oliver — 151st Inf. Bde. Bombing Officer 22/2/15.

2/Lieut. O.J. Feetham — 150th Inf. Bde 29/7/16. To Duty 23/10/16.

2/Lieut. J.R. Percy. — Wounded 17/7/16. To England 22/7/15. Rejoined Bn. 7/10/15.

2/Lieut. R.W. Marley — T/Lieut. 26/6/15. 151st M.G. Coy. seconded 6/2/16.

Joined Bn. 30/7/15.

2/Lieut. L. Ewbank. — Killed in action 23/2/16.

Commissioned from ranks of this Battalion.

2/Lieut. C.E. Pass — Proceeded to join 2/5th Bn. Border Regt. 10/9/15. Rejoined Bn. 3/3/16. To England 5/9/16.

Joined Bn. 22/9/15 from 5th Royal Berks Regt. as Comdg. Officer.

Major W.R.P. Kemmis-Betty — To England 26/10/15.

Joined Bn. 6/10/15.

Lieut. G.J. Monson-Fitzjohn — To R.F.C. 16/1/16. Seconded 11/3/16.

Joined Bn. 1/11/15.

2/Lieut. H.P. Rhind — To England 11/3/16. Rejoined Bn. 19/10/16

Joined Bn. 2/11/15.

2/Lieut G. Hill — To England 15/1/16.

Joined Bn. 11/11/15 from 6th Bn. N.F. as Commanding Officer.

Major J.R. Hedley, D.S.O. — T/Lt.Col 11/11/15.

Joined Bn. 24/12/15.

2/Lieut. J.A. Stout — T/Lt. 7/2/16.

Joined Bn. 3/1/16.

2/Lieut. G.H. Dawes — T/Lieut. 23/2/16. Killed in action 16/9/16.

Joined Bn.12/2/16. from 2nd Bn. Royal Scots as Adjutant.

Lieut.J.H.Martin   To England 2 4/6/16. Rejoined 26/9/16.

Joined Bn.13/2/16.

2/Lieut.J.P. Bennett   Wounded 25/5/16. To England 1/6/16.
                       Rejoined Bn. 13/8/16.

Joined Bn.14/8/16.

2/Lieut.A.L.Ford   To 150th Inf.Bde. 25/10/16.

2/Lieut A.G.Condi   Killed in action 1/10/16.

Joined Bn.16/3/16.

2/Lieut.C.R.Suiter   Seconded for duty with 151 T.M.Bty. 25/5/16.

Joined Bn.3/5/16. from Cadet School, G.H.Q.

2/Lieut.J.Mackay   Wounded 25/5/16. To England 5/6/16.

2/Lieut E.J.Pursglove Wounded 1/6/16. To England 4/6/16.
                       Rejoined Bn.13/8/16. Wounded 16/9/16.
                       To England 18/9/16.

2/Lieut.J.S.Booth   To M.G.Training Centre Grantham and
                       struck off strength 5/9/16.

Joined Bn. 11/5/16.

2/Lieut.H.B. Beaumont

Joined Bn. 12/5/16.

2/Lieut.H.Bell

Joined Bn. 18/5/16. 10th Middlesex Regiment.

2/Lieut.H.Pride

2/Lieut.L.O.Stoken   Wounded 25/5/16. To England 4/6/16.

Joined Bn.19/5/16.

2/Lieut.A.Feetham   Killed in action 18/9/16.

2/Lieut. H.Hutchinson

Joined Bn.2/6/16.

Lt.& Q.M. M. Davies.

Joined Bn. 5/6/16.

2/Lieut.C.W.Fagan.

Joined Bn.10/6/16.

2/Lieut.F.J.Lain   Wounded 16/9/16. To England 21/9/16.

2/Lieut. S.E.MacGowan To England 14/9/16.

WAR DIARY.
5 BORDER REGT.
NOVEMBER, 1916.
VOLUME 12.

Army Form C. 2118.

WAR DIARY
or
INTELLIGENCE SUMMARY.
(Erase heading not required.)

Place	Date	Hour	Summary of Events and Information	Remarks and references to Appendices
	1-11-16 to 2-11-16		The Battalion carried on with road making and fatigues. The following is an extract taken from 50th Division Routine Orders dated 1-11-16:- The Army Commander has awarded the following decoration to the undermentioned N.C.O.:- 2345 Sgt H. Bowen, 5/ The Border Regt: and 15/st French Mortar Battery:- MILITARY MEDAL.	772
	3-11-16		The Battalion proceeded to DROP ALLEY and FLERS LINE and relieved the 7th Battalion Northumberland Fusiliers.	
	4-11-16		Two Companies moved forward to ABBAYE TRENCH. Bn. Hd. Qrs. moved to HEXHAM ROAD.	
	5-11-16	At 9.10 a.m. (ZERO HOUR)	"A" Company moved from its present position and occupied the SNAG TRENCH and SNAG SUPPORT vacated by the 8th Bn. Durham Light Infantry who had moved forward to the attack. "B" Company remained in its present position ready to move at ZERO HOUR awaiting orders.	
		10:	Companies and the Bombers moved to HEXHAM ROAD (M.23.d., Sheet 57c S.W.) taking up positions before 8.45 a.m. The above positions were reconnoitred by Company Commanders immediately	

WAR DIARY or INTELLIGENCE SUMMARY

Army Form C. 2118.

Place	Date	Hour	Summary of Events and Information	Remarks and references to Appendices
	6.11.16		After dawn with a view to obtaining the best cover got their men. Attack of 8th/9th D.L.I. proved unsuccessful and they were withdrawn to support line, being relieved by the Battalion. "A" and "B" Companies continued to hold the front line (SNAG TRENCH) each having three platoons there and one platoon each in SNAG SUPPORT. "C" Company were stopped along the SNAG SUPPORT and down SNAG TRENCH to the left. "D" Company remaining in ABBAYE TRENCH. The Battalion was relieved on the night of 6/7th by the 4th East Yorks and Companies marched back independently to the Camp near MAMETZ WOOD.	
	7.11.16		The Battalion supplied large working and carrying parties daily, extending the whole Battalion at road making.	
	do		The Camp was greatly improved, drains dug and shell holes filled in. Trench boards were laid and chalk walks there made.	
	15.11.16		The following message was received from 151st Infantry Brigade:- "Captain W.B. Little, Staff Captain, 151st Infantry Brigade appointed 2nd in Command	

WAR DIARY
or
INTELLIGENCE SUMMARY.

Army Form C. 2118.

Place	Date	Hour	Summary of Events and Information	Remarks and references to Appendices
	16-11-16		5th Bn. The Border Regiment from 10th November 1916. Major A.C. Scanlar rejoined Battalion on the 14th inst. The 151st Infantry Brigade was relieved by the 3rd Infantry Brigade today, the former less 6th Bn. D.L.I, 8th Bn. D.L.I. and this Battalion proceeded to MIRVENCOURT, on relief. The Battalions mentioned being left for road making.	
	17-11-16		The Battalion took over the work previously done by the 1st Royal Munster Fusiliers on the roads as stated:- One Company at KANGLAND CIRCUS, S.14.c.1.8., one at S.14.c.1.9., one at S.20.c.2.8., one at S.25.c.6.4. and another, called HQ Company at S.20.a.3.8. Two officers per company and every available man were employed daily. A fifth Company being made up of sub-units called HQ Company. Companies paraded at 6 a.m. commencing their work at 6.30 a.m. and finishing about 3 p.m.	Ref. Supp. Sheet 5 & 5a
	do		The following is an extract from 50th Division Routine Order dated 20-11-16:- The Corps Commander has awarded the following decorations do	
	30-11-16			

774

WAR DIARY
or
INTELLIGENCE SUMMARY.
(Erase heading not required.)

Army Form C. 2118.

Place	Date	Hour	Summary of Events and Information	Remarks and references to Appendices
	30/11/16		The undermentioned men:- 1685 Pte G. Allison, 5/ The Border Regt. and 151st Trench Mortar Battery – MILITARY MEDAL Extract taken from 50th Division Routine Orders dated 28/11/16:- "The Corps Commander has awarded the following decorations to the undermentioned men:- 2241 Pte J. Ferguson, 5/ The Border Regiment – MILITARY MEDAL Battalion ceased work at 2 p.m., an hour earlier than usual and returned to Camp. to collect kits. The Battalion paraded at 3.30 p.m. and proceeded to a Camp near BECOURT (F.1. & 9.7.) arriving about 5.45 p.m. where they rested for the night.	

J. H. Martin Lieut. Adjt.
for O.C. 5th Bn. The Border Regt.
1.12.16.

Nov 15

WAR DIARY
5th Bn. The Border Regt.
30th November
31st December

VOLUME No. 13

Army Form C. 2118.

WAR DIARY
or
INTELLIGENCE SUMMARY.
(Erase heading not required.)

Instructions regarding War Diaries and Intelligence Summaries are contained in F. S. Regs., Part II. and the Staff Manual respectively. Title pages will be prepared in manuscript.

Place	Date	Hour	Summary of Events and Information	Remarks and references to Appendices
	1/12/16		The Battalion paraded at 9.20 a.m. moved off at 9.20 a.m. and marched to WARLOY via ALBERT – MILLENCOURT and HENENCOURT having dinner en route. Arrived at WARLOY and alloted billets.	
	2,3/12/16		Spent in generally clearing up of billets, rifles, equipment, clothing &c.	
	4/12/16		Spent in Squad, Platoon, Company and Battalion training.	
	to		Sundays – Church Parades and generally cleaning up. The following is a copy of letter received from Brigadier General, III Corps:- "The Corps Commander wishes to place on record his great appreciation of the work done by the troops on the roads, railways and tramways during the last six weeks, in the III Corps Area under adverse weather conditions. He fully realizes the great amount of extra labour it thus involved, and hopes that all ranks will realize how essential the work was in view of future operations and further got their own welfare."	
	26/12/16		On the 10th inst. the G.O.C. 151st Infantry Brigade presented medal ribbons to the undermentioned of the Battalion:-	

WAR DIARY
or
INTELLIGENCE SUMMARY.

Place	Date	Hour	Summary of Events and Information	Remarks and references to Appendices
	28.12.16		Distinguished Conduct Medal. 1483 Sgt. N. Bradbury. 3354 Cpl. J. Slater. Military Medal. 1299 Sgt. J. James, 2134 Sgt. W. Swan, 1417 Sgt. J. Travis, 2891 L/C. W. B. Burke, 2055 Pte. W.S. Wilson, 1542 Pte. J. Deaton, 2231 Pte. R. Banks, 2241 Pte. J. Ferguson. The Battalion was relieved by a Battalion of the 143rd Infantry Brigade and marched to ALBERT and relieved the 7th Bn. Royal Warwickshire Regiment.	
	30.12.16		At 9.30 A.M. the Battalion left ALBERT and marched to a camp north of MAMETZ WOOD (S.14.a.3.4., Sheet 57c. S.W.) and relieved the 1st Northampton--shire Regiment.	
	31.12.16		The Battalion relieved the 2nd K.R.R. Corps in the support line at M.30.c.4.2. (in support of 9th R.I.) leaving camp at 3.30 p.m. in	

Army Form C. 2118.

WAR DIARY
or
INTELLIGENCE SUMMARY.

(Erase heading not required.)

Place	Date	Hour	Summary of Events and Information	Remarks and references to Appendices
			The following orders Hd. Qrs. 'B' 'C' D and 'A' Companies relief being completed at 7 p.m.	

J. Ashworth Capt
fr O.C. 5th Bn Somt
21-7-16

York 151/50

WAR DIARY.

5th Bn. The Border Regiment.

January 1917.

Volume No. 18.

Army Form C. 2118.

WAR DIARY
or
INTELLIGENCE SUMMARY.
(Erase heading not required.)

Instructions regarding War Diaries and Intelligence Summaries are contained in F. S. Regs., Part II and the Staff Manual respectively. Title pages will be prepared in manuscript.

Place	Date	Hour	Summary of Events and Information	Remarks and references to Appendices
	4-1-17		The Battalion was relieved by the 1st Bn Durham L. Inf. and returned to HIGH WOOD WEST CAMP in reserve.	
	8-1-17		Relieved the 8th Bn Durham L. Inf. in the front line	
	10-1-17		Relieved by the 6th Bn Durham R. Inf. and returned to BAZENTIN CAMP SITE. 5. in reserve.	
	16-1-17		Relieved the 8th Bn Durham L. Inf. in the Support Line	
	20-1-17		Relieved by the 6th Bn Durham L. Inf. and returned to BAZENTIN CAMP SITE. 1. in reserve.	
	24-1-17		Relieved 8th Bn Durham L. Inf. in front line. The Battn were employed as above, 4 days in the front line Support and four days in Camp in Reserve. Nothing unusual happened during the month. The Battalion's work consisted of strengthening and improving the position when the line and cleaning and draining of Camps when out. Carrying and fatigue parties were also supplied by the Battalion when in Support and Reserve.	
	26-1-17		The Battalion was relieved by the 8th Bn Australian Infantry and went back into BAZENTIN CAMP SITE. 3.	
	27-1-17		The Battalion paraded at 8.45 am and marched to BECOURT CAMP. H. arriving there about 11.0 am.	
	28-1-17		Camp fatigues only were supplied.	
	29-1-17		The Battalion paraded at 11-20 am and marched to RIBEMONT.	

Army Form C. 2118.

WAR DIARY
or
INTELLIGENCE SUMMARY.
(Erase heading not required.)

Instructions regarding War Diaries and Intelligence Summaries are contained in F. S. Regs. Part II. and the Staff Manual respectively. Title pages will be prepared in manuscript.

Place	Date	Hour	Summary of Events and Information	Remarks and references to Appendices
	29/1/17		VIA ALBERT. Main Road, Cross Roads. (D.16.a.3.4.) (Sheet 62.D.) arriving at RIBEMONT. at 3.0 p.m.	
	30/1/17		The day was spent in generally cleaning up of Rifles, Equipment, Clothing &c.	
	31/1/17		Platoon and Company drill, cleaning up billets and sanitary work.	

J Atkinson Lt Col
for OC 5th Border Regt.

Army Form C. 2118.

WAR DIARY
or
INTELLIGENCE SUMMARY.
(Erase heading not required.)

WAR DIARY.
5th Bn. The Border Regt.
February 1917.
Volume 14.

VOLUME 14.

Army Form C. 2118.

WAR DIARY
or
INTELLIGENCE SUMMARY.

(Erase heading not required.)

Instructions regarding War Diaries and Intelligence Summaries are contained in F. S. Regs., Part II. and the Staff Manual respectively. Title pages will be prepared in manuscript.

Place	Date	Hour	Summary of Events and Information	Remarks and references to Appendices
RIBEMONT.	1/4 34y	—	During this period the Battalion carried out tactical exercises. each Company in turn spent one day on the rifle range and bombing pits.	
"	5th		The whole Battn took part in a Brigade Route march. ROUTE:- RIBEMONT.– BAIZIEUX– FRAMVILLIERS– RIBEMONT.	
"	6th		Brigade scheme and usual inspections were carried out before moving to relieve the French Army in Divisional new area.	
"	10th		The Battalion marched to MORCOURT. Route via CERISY, where a halt was made for the day.	
MORCOURT.	11th		The Battalion paraded in mass for Commanding Officers inspection afterwards carrying out apractice attack.	
"	12th		The Battalion completed its move into the new area, marching from MORCOURT via PROYART to hutments at BOIS. ST MARTIN, where it relieved the 5th Bn Yorks Regt 150 Inf Bde who went in Divisional Reserve.	
BOIS. ST MARTIN.	12th /18		Whilst in Divisional Reserve the Battalion furnished working parties. The work chiefly consisted of carrying and owing to chan much difficulty was experienced by these parties.	
FAUCAUCOURT	19th		The Battalion relieved the 6th Bn D.L.I. in Brigade Reserve and marched to hutments at CAMP– POMIERS. FAUCAUCOURT. Carrying parties were furnished by the Battalion during the period in Reserve.	
	23rd /24		The Battalion relieved the 6th Bn D.L.I. in the front line A.D.C. Corp	

Army Form C. 2118.

WAR DIARY
or
INTELLIGENCE SUMMARY.
(Erase heading not required.)

Instructions regarding War Diaries and Intelligence Summaries are contained in F. S. Regs., Part II. and the Staff Manual respectively. Title pages will be prepared in manuscript.

Place	Date	Hour	Summary of Events and Information	Remarks and references to Appendices
	24/8.		in fire trenches. "B" Company and Special Unit occupying the support lines. Owing to thaw the ground was in a treacherous state, thus causing relief to be late. Period spent in front line much work was spent in at. improving conditions in the line, which owing to the wet weather, and thaw were in the worst possible condition. The Battalion was relieved this evening by the 18/H.L.I. and moved into Brigade Reserve at BERNY, relief on this occasion was completed in good time.	

J.R. Hedley
Lieut. Col.

Army Form C. 2118.

WAR DIARY
INTELLIGENCE SUMMARY.
(Erase heading not required.)

5th Bn. The Border Regt.
March 1917.
Volume 15.

5th Battalion
THE BORDER REGIMENT

WAR DIARY or INTELLIGENCE SUMMARY

Army Form C. 2118.

Volume 15

MARCH 1917

Place	Date	Hour	Summary of Events and Information	Remarks and references to Appendices
Berry	1.		The Battalion was in Brigade Reserve and during the 4 days supplied large working parties (wiring revetting).	
	4-5		The Battalion moved into the left sub section relieving the 6th Bn. D.L.I & 7th Bn moving into the left trenches, "B" Coy in the centre, "B" Coy on the right and "A" Coy in outpost in Forest Trench. During this tour of duty much work was done in repairing and cleaning of trenches which owing to wet weather were in a very bad condition.	
	7-8		The Battalion was relieved by the 6th Bn. North Staff Regt 59th Division and moved into Camp POMMIERS - FOUCAUCOURT. Relief was completed in good time considering the distance and weather conditions.	
	8.		The Battalion reached the night of 7/8th at Foucaucourt and paraded at 1.30pm on 8th for Cos. inspection preparatory to moving to MERRICOURT SUR SOMME, made via Main AMIENS ROAD - PROYART arriving at the destination about 4 p.m.	
	9-14		This time was spent in the general clearing up of arms, equipment, clothing etc. Platoon Company training was commenced, also training of specialists was being companied. Rifle range and bombing pits were also under construction each company in turn supplied a working party of 1 Officer and 50 men until same was completed.	
	16-24		Battalion training and recreational training during the afternoon	

Army Form C. 2118.

WAR DIARY
or
INTELLIGENCE SUMMARY.

(Erase heading not required.)

Instructions regarding War Diaries and Intelligence Summaries are contained in F. S. Regs., Part II. and the Staff Manual respectively. Title pages will be prepared in manuscript.

Place	Date	Hour	Summary of Events and Information	Remarks and references to Appendices
	16/27th		was carried out. Training of Specialists continued during this period. Four entries were made in the Divisional Transport to competition, when one of our travelling Field Kitchens was awarded the 1st Prize in 2nd class also the Divisional Championship Prize for the best turnout.	
	28th		The Battalion paraded at 9.15 a.m. and marched to MORCOURT to be inspected and addressed by the Corps Commander (Lt. Genl. Sir W.P. Pulteney. K.C.B. C.M.V. D.S.O.) Training continued.	
	29. 30th			
	31st		The Battalion paraded at 7.45 am and marched to K.9 central 6.2.D. (embussing point) where they embussed and were conveyed to TALMAS. The move being completed by 3.9pm.	

A. Cow
Worsley
for O.C. 5th Bn. The Border Regt.

WAR DIARY No. 19
5th Bn The 12th FF Regt

Volume 16
for
APRIL 1944

Army Form C. 2118.

WAR DIARY
or
INTELLIGENCE SUMMARY.
(Erase heading not required.)

April 1917.

Place	Date	Hour	Summary of Events and Information	Remarks and references to Appendices
TALMAS	April 1st		Battalion remained at TALMAS. Church parade was held and a short route march made.	
"	2nd	7.30am	Battalion marched to GEZAINCOURT.	
GEZAINCOURT	3rd	7.10am	Battalion marched to P.T and GND BOURIET SUR CANCHE.	
G. BOURIET	4th	8.15am	Battalion marched HD.Qrs and 1 Coy to SIRACOURT, remaining 3 Coys to BEAUVIES.	
SIRACOURT	5th		Battalion remained at above two lines places. The C.O. visits the O.Ps.	
"	6th		in ARRAS together with the Brigade Staff and the other Battalion Commanders. Orders received to move to TERNAS but these were cancelled later. The C.O. 2/Cmd and a detachment attended the funeral of Major HUNT 6th D.L.I. at ST POL.	
"	7th	10.30am	Battalion marches to TERNAS.	
TERNAS	8th	10.30am	Battalion marched to IZEL-LEZ-HAMEAU. A Coy proceeds KABIGNY on fatigue-work, unloading supply trains.	
TERNAS	9th		Practice in attack carried out by Coys.	

5/ THE BORDER REGT

VOLUME 16.

Army Form C. 2118.

Instructions regarding War Diaries and Intelligence
Summaries are contained in F. S. Regs., Part II.
and the Staff Manual respectively. Title pages
will be prepared in manuscript.

WAR DIARY
or
INTELLIGENCE SUMMARY.

(Erase heading not required.)

April 1917

Place	Date	Hour	Summary of Events and Information	Remarks and references to Appendices
TERNAS	10th	At 1 a.m.	orders received to be prepared to move at short notice	
"	"	3 pm	Battalion less D. Coy marches to GOUVES.	
GOUVES	11th	5 pm	Battalion less D. Coy marched to FBG D'RONVILLE (ARRAS) and relieved the 6th Bn K.O.Y.L.I. in Billets.	
			During the whole of the march from the SOMME to ARRAS the weather was bitterly cold with frost and snow daily.	
RONVILLE	12th		During the afternoon the C.O. visited TELEGRAPH HILL.	
		5.30 p.m	Battalion less D. Coy moved to position about 1000 yds N of NEUVILLE VITASSE.	
		5.30 pm	D. Coy rejoined Bn having marched from AUBIGNY via GOUVES. About 6.30pm a hostile shell struck one of D. Coys billets killing 5 O.R.s and wounding 6.	
	13th	5 am	D. Coy moved up and rejoined Battalion.	
	14th		Early next morning the Battalion moved into the bed of the COJEUL RIVER to support an attack delivered by the 6th D.L.I.	

Army Form C. 2118.

WAR DIARY
or
INTELLIGENCE SUMMARY.
(Erase heading not required.)

April 1917

Instructions regarding War Diaries and Intelligence Summaries are contained in F. S. Regs., Part II. and the Staff Manual respectively. Title pages will be prepared in manuscript.

Place	Date	Hour	Summary of Events and Information	Remarks and references to Appendices
	14th	contd.	The area was shelled considerably but very few casualties incurred. At dusk the Bn. withdrew to THE HARP – S.of TILLOY. C.Coy was detailed to assist the 9th D.L.I. to dig in near WANCOURT TOWER.	
	15th		During the afternoon the Bn. returned to THE CAVES – ARRAS – having been relieved by the 4th EAST YORKS.	
THE CAVES, ARRAS	16th 17th 18th 19th 20th		The Battalion remained in THE CAVES, various working parties were supplied.	
	21st		Battalion moved up to THE HARP. in support.	
	22nd		Battalion remained in support.	
	23rd	4-45pm	Battalion moved to NEPAL TRENCH. Bt the hour the 150th I.B. attacked and took the objective about 1000 yds. E. of WANCOURT TOWER but were driven back at midday by a strong counter attack delivered by the enemy.	

WAR DIARY or INTELLIGENCE SUMMARY

Army Form C. 2118.

April 1917

Place	Date	Hour	Summary of Events and Information	Remarks and references to Appendices
Cojeul	23rd		B. & C. Coys were ordered to move to N 24 c.0.5. to draw Knife rests to places in front of the O.G. trench and then consolidate them but owing to the counterattack on the 15th I.B. they were kept at THE BANK about N24.c.0.5. At 6 p.m. the Battalion with the 9th D.L.I. on the left, attacked and retook the objective 5 Heavy T.Gs several T.Ms and about 200 prisoners were captured also many of our wounded taken in the enemy counter attack were recovered. (150" I.B.) In our attack B. Coy remained in Echelon to defend the flank as the division on our right did not reach its objective. A platoon of the left Coy. D. got well forward + occupies front of an old German trench and were subsequently absorbed by the 9th D.L.I. where orders they remained until time of Bn relief.	
	24th		At 4 p.m. The Bn before attack but was held up by enemy artillery & M.G. fire. At dusk another attack which proved successful was launched. The objective was reached and a line dug and consolidated. During these operations 6 Officers were killed 94 wounded, Cornallis 9 O.R.s were to follow R.45, W.131. M. wounded R. 23.	

Army Form C. 2118.

WAR DIARY
or
INTELLIGENCE SUMMARY.   April 1917.
(Erase heading not required.)

Instructions regarding War Diaries and Intelligence Summaries are contained in F. S. Regs., Part II and the Staff Manual respectively. Title pages will be prepared in manuscript.

Place	Date	Hour	Summary of Events and Information	Remarks and references to Appendices
	25th		The Battn was relieved in the line by the 9th R.B. and returned to the Sunken Road about N.14.A.	
	26th	9.30 am	Battalion returned to Billets in RONVILLE.	
	27th		Battalion moved to Billets in ARRAS and during the evening returned to Rest Area - COULLEMONT.	
	28th 29th 30th		Battalion resting in Billets.	

Vol 20

WAR DIARY
The Border Regt.
5th Bn
Volume 17
MAY, 1917

5th BATT.N THE BORDER REGIMENT.

Army Form C. 2118.

Instructions regarding War Diaries and Intelligence
Summaries are contained in F. S. Regs. Part II.
and the Staff Manual respectively. Title pages
will be prepared in manuscript.

WAR DIARY
or
INTELLIGENCE SUMMARY.
(Erase heading not required.)

VOLUME 17. MAY 1917.

Place	Date	Hour	Summary of Events and Information	Remarks and references to Appendices
	May 1		The Battn moved by march route to POMMIER Area, being billeted at BERLES AU BOIS.	
	2		The Battn moved to BELLACOURT where it remained for 2 days.	
	4		Orders were received for the Brigade to move back to the COUTURELLE Area, the Battn marched to COULLEMONT and occupied same billets as on previous occasion.	
	5/17		The Battn was in Corps Reserve. This period was spent in the cleaning of equipment etc. and Battn & Brigade Training.	
	18		The Battn moved by march route to MONCHY AU BOIS where it was bivouacked. Battalion Sports.	
	19/20		The time was spent in training, night manoeuvres being carried out.	
	20/23		The Battn moved by march route to ST. AMAND.	
	24		During this period training was carried out.	
	25/31		On the 26th inst the G.O.C. 151st Inf. Bde. Brigadier General N.J.G. Cameron, C.M.G. presented ribbons to the recipients of awards recently made.	

J R Hedley
Lieut. Col. ? Comdg

Army Form C. 2118.

WAR DIARY
or
INTELLIGENCE SUMMARY.
(Erase heading not required.)

WAR DIARY.

5th Bn. The Border Regiment, T.F.

June 1917.

Volume 18.

5th BORDER REGIMENT

WAR DIARY or INTELLIGENCE SUMMARY.
(Erase heading not required.)

Army Form C. 2118.

VOLUME 18.

June 1917.

Place	Date	Hour	Summary of Events and Information	Remarks and references to Appendices
	1/13		The Battn continued its training in the St. AMAND Area. Musketry, general instruction and manœuvres (night) were carried out	
	14		Orders were received to move into the forward Area. These Orders were cancelled later, the Battn standing by.	
	15		Orders were received to move forward by march route via MONCHY AU BOIS, ADINFER where a halt was made until the cool of the evening. The march was resumed at 6.30 by way of BOISLEUX AU MONT to Bivouacs at HENIN-SUR-COJEUL.	
	16/19		During this time the Battn was in Reserve instruction was carried out in wiring, and bad shots carried out special practices on Rifle Range. The Battn moved into support trenches south of WANCOURT TOWER. The Battn relieved the 8th Bn D.L.I. During the four days spent here, practically the whole Battn was employed on working parties, either for front line work or for R.E.	
	19/20		The Battn was relieved by the 6th Bn N.F. and Companies moved independently to Camp near BOISLEUX AU MONT by route of HENINEL, ST. MARTIN-SUR-COJEUL and BOISLEUX ST. MARK.	
	23/24			
	24/28		The Battn was employed in general training, cleaning of arms and equipment and preparing for G.O.C. Inspection.	

Army Form C. 2118.

WAR DIARY
or
INTELLIGENCE SUMMARY.

(Erase heading not required.)

June 1917

Place	Date	Hour	Summary of Events and Information	Remarks and references to Appendices
	29		The Battn. was inspected by Major-General Sir P.S. Wilkinson, K.C.M.G., C.B., D.S.O., (Commanding 50th. Northumbrian. Division).	
	30		The day was spent in general inspection of arms & equipment.	

R.B. Davitt -

WAR DIARY:- YK22

5TH BN THE BORDER REGT

JULY 1917

VOLUME No XIX

TAPE PARTY

This party will lay out tape from point of assembly to point of entry into the enemy trench & on return must if not is at all possible drag in the tape with them.

IDENTIFICATION

All marks of identification even to identity discs will be left behind & each officer & man will be provided with a number a duplicate of which will be kept at Bn Hqrs together with the man's name allotted to the number, on return all numbers will be collected & forwarded to Headquarters for checking.

PATROLLING

Before the part moves off 2/Lt Laidlaw will make a reconnaissance of the ground to be covered & assure himself that all is clear to advance.

Operation Orders By
Major E.J. Crouch DSO
Comdg 5th Bn The Border Regt

7/5

Ref Map.
Mercara Nº 12

General Idea.
On the night of the 8th Aug. 1917 the 5th Border Regt will carry out a raid on the enemy trenches from O 26 c 5 8½ to O 26 a 6 .4

Special Idea.
The raiding party will consist of 3 parties i.e. Right & Left Raiding Parties + a covering party; the whole under the command of Capt. J.L. Henderson + will be organised as follows.

Right Party.	Left Party.
2/Lt J.C. Laidlaw	2/Lt E.I. Hall
Bombing Squad 1 NCO + 4 men	Composition
Nº 1 Clearing " "	of Left Party as
" 2	for right except,
" 3	of tape party
Parapet Party " "	which will act
Tape Party 1 NCO + 1 man	for the 2 parties

and 4 Stretcher Bearers will move forward in rear of the raiding party & will remain at a point about O.26.c 4.1½ + supervise as far as possible the advance & withdrawal of the raiding party.

The advance of the raiding party from the point of assembly O.26.c.5.9½ point of entry into the enemy trenches will be in two small parallel snake columns in file, touch must be maintained so that both columns can work in cohesion.

Zero Hour

Zero hour will be at 10.45 p.m. at which time the party will enter the enemy trenches.

Fixed belts of overhead M.G. fire will be opened & Stokes Guns & Trench Mortars will fire on selected targets, the opening of fire will announce to the party raiding that zero hour has arrived.

Zero plus 10 minutes the party will withdraw from the enemy trench by the "Stand fast" being blown on the bugle.

DRESS Dress for the raiding party will be clean fatigue with soft caps.

Cont

box respirators with Alert position magazines will be charged, bayonets fixed & sand bag lightly covering bayonet. 15 rds of ammn will be carried in the pocket & two Mills bombs. Faces & hands will be blackened with burnt cork

Watches   Watches will be synchronised at 12 noon & one hour before Zero.

Tools   Every man must be provided with wire cutters. Parapet Party will carry two shovels with each party & immediately raiding party has entered enemy trench will commence to fill it in to assist quick withdrawal of party, this party will also carry a fast loading rope.

Prisoners   will be handed over to the Parapet party who will guard them until the party withdraws. Every man must be taught the German for "Hands Up". Prisoners shall be forwarded handed over to the Parapet party who will guard them until the party withdraws. Prisoners will be forwarded with all possible speed to Bn Hqrs.

Covering Party.
    Capt. J. L. Henderson
        Lewis Gun + Team 1 NCO – 6
        Riflemen   1 – 5
        Buglers   2
        Stretcher Bearers   4

The party will leave our trenches at 0.26 a 2½ three quarters of an hour before zero hour and assemble behind the sky line. The bearing for the advance will be 105°. The point of entry into the enemy trenches will be at 0.26 d 5 - 9½.

The covering party will be posted in position prior to the advance of the raiding party in sufficient time to allow the raiding party to advance ¾ hour before zero hour in the following positions.

1 Lewis Gun + team of 1 NCO + 6 men of which 5 will be riflemen at 0.26 a 6.3 to cover the left flank + deal with any machine guns on North of O.26 a 6.1 to O 26 a 10.3.

The riflemen will occupy a position at about O.26 c 3.9 + cover the left right flank

    Capt J. L. Henderson with 2 buglers

5th Bn THE BORDER REGT.

Army Form C. 2118.

WAR DIARY
or
INTELLIGENCE SUMMARY.

(Erase heading not required.)

VOLUME. 19.   JULY 1917

Instructions regarding War Diaries and Intelligence Summaries are contained in F.S. Regs., Part II. and the Staff Manual respectively. Title pages will be prepared in manuscript.

Place	Date	Hour	Summary of Events and Information	Remarks and references to Appendices
	1st		The Battn. was camped near BOISLEUX-AU-MONT.	
	2/3rd		On the night of 2/3rd the Battn. moved into forward area relieving the 4th London Regt. (Royal Fusiliers) in the Left Sub Sector.	
	4/6th		During this tour of duty much work was done in improving the trenches occupied.	
	6/7th		The Battn. was relieved by the 8th Bn. D.L.I. and moved into Reserve Area about N.20.a.+c. (51.B.S.M.) Many working parties were furnished and relief was late.	
	8/10th		During this period large working parties were found by the Battn. for the carrying of R.E. material. During the daytime inspections of arms, equipment, clothing etc. were carried out preparatory to moving into Front Line.	
	10/11th		The Battn. moved into the Front Line relieving the 8th D.L.I. in the Left Sector. The disposition of the Battn. was as follows:-	
			'A' Coy Right Front Sub Sector	
			'B' " Left Front Sub Sector } GUEMMAPPE
			'C' " In Support Area CAVALRY, KEY + LOCK Trenches.	
			'D' " Occupying Reserve Area RAKE TRENCH.	
			Much work was done in the trenches occupied during this period.	
	14/15th		The Battn. was relieved by 8th Battn. D.L.I. and moved into Support area at MARLIERE.	

Army Form C. 2118.

WAR DIARY
or
INTELLIGENCE SUMMARY.
(Erase heading not required.)

Instructions regarding War Diaries and Intelligence Summaries are contained in F. S. Regs., Part II. and the Staff Manual respectively. Title pages will be prepared in manuscript.

Place	Date	Hour	Summary of Events and Information	Remarks and references to Appendices
	15th		Sudden death of Lieut. Col. J.R. Hedley. D.S.O. from natural causes (heart disease) Lieut. Col. J.R. Hedley. D.S.O. had been in command of the 5th Battn. The Border Regt. from the 11th November 1915 up to this date. On the night of 14/15th July he came down from the Battn. Hd. Qrs in the line to the Transport lines with the intention of taking over temporary command of the 151st Infy. Bde. in which he was senior Battalion commander, during the absence of the Brigadier General Commander on duty. He died about 9 a.m. at the Transport lines. Lieut. Col. Hedley's death came as a great shock to all officers and men of his Battalion, by whom he was beloved for his courage, strong sense of justice and his genial disposition.	
	16th		Burial of Lieut. Col. J.R. Hedley. D.S.O. at MILITARY CEMETERY S.2.6.88. 51.B.S.W. Amongst those present at the service were Major General Sir P.S. Wilkinson. K.C.M.G. D.S.O. commanding 50th Division and Brigadier General N.J.G. Cameron. C.M.G. D.S.O. commanding the 151st Infy. Bde.	
	17th		Working parties were again furnished by the Battn.	
	18/19th		The Battn. was relieved by 5th Bn. N. Fusiliers. (149th Infy Bde.) and moved into Divisional Reserve occupying camp of the latter Battn. at N.26.c.1.6. Sheet 61.B. S.W.	

A.5834 Wt.W4973/M687 750,000 8/16 D. D. & L. Ltd. Forms/C.2118/13.

Army Form C. 2118.

WAR DIARY
or
INTELLIGENCE SUMMARY.
(Erase heading not required.)

Instructions regarding War Diaries and Intelligence Summaries are contained in F. S. Regs., Part II. and the Staff Manual respectively. Title pages will be prepared in manuscript.

Place	Date	Hour	Summary of Events and Information	Remarks and references to Appendices
	20/26th		This period was spent in Musketry Practice. Training and night operations were carried out.	
	27/28th		The Battn. moved from Divisional Reserve (being relieved by 5th Bn. D.L.I. 150th Bde.) into the Front Line, relieving the other Battn. in the Left Sub Sector as follows. 'C' Coy. Right Front Coy. 'D' " Left Front Coy. 'B' " Right Support Coy. 'A' " Left Support Coy. } CHERISY.	
	29/30th		Much work was done in improving Trenches occupied.	
	31st		The Battn. was relieved by 6th Bn. D.L.I. and passed into Bde. Reserve, occupying camp at N.26.c.1.o. near HENIN.	

WAR DIARY or INTELLIGENCE SUMMARY.

Army Form C. 2118.

Place	Date	Hour	Summary of Events and Information	Remarks and references to Appendices
			The undermentioned Officers were struck off the strength of the Battalion during this month. Lieut. Col. J.R. Stedley. D.S.O. (died), Capt. A.D. Soulsby, Lieut. A.J. Ford, 2/Lt. J.P. Bennett. The undermentioned Officers and Other Ranks joined the Battalion for duty. Major E.H. Branch. D.S.O. 9th D.L.I. (attached) Capt. L. Rigg. Lt. & Q.m. W. Benwick. appointed Q.m. 15 Other Ranks from England 14 Other Ranks returned from base.	

J Thomson Lt-Col
1st O.C.
5th Bn. The Border Regt.

Vol 23

151/50

WAR DIARY

5th Bn Rowan Regiment

August 1917

VOLUME - XIX

WAR DIARY
of
INTELLIGENCE SUMMARY.

(Erase heading not required.)

VOLUME 20   5TH BATTN THE BORDER REGT.   Army Form C. 2118.

AUGUST 1917

Place	Date	Hour	Summary of Events and Information	Remarks and references to Appendices
	1/3rd		The Battn. remained in Brigade Reserve in Camp N.26.C.I.O. HENIN. Training was much restricted by heavy rains.	
	4th		Commencing at 7 a.m. the Battn. relieved the 9th Bn L.N. in support Battn. Area (CHERISY Sector) Relief was completed at 9 a.m.	
	5th		Commencing at 2.0 pm on the same afternoon, the Battn. moved into front line trenches (same sector) relieving the 9th Bn L.N. Relief was completed at 5.0 pm and Coys were distributed as follows :- 'B' Coy Right Front, 'A' Coy Left Front, 'D' Coy Support, 'C' Coy Reserve. In the evening 'A' Coy handed over frontage from BIG SAP inclusive to 0.26.a.4.2. to the 4th Bn E. Yorks Regt. Right Front Battn of the Brigade on left, on completion of relief the garrison of the Posts relieved, withdrew to BULLFINCH SUPPORT.	
	6th		The following readjustment of Battn. frontage was made by over-lapping to the right, commencing at 10 am 'A' Coy relieved four Posts of 'B' Coy from 9th Bn L.N. 'B' Coy took over from 9th Bn L.N. from LONE SAP inclusive. 'B' Coy on their right. 'B' Coy relieved one Coy of 9th Bn L.N. from LONE SAP to WREN LANE inclusive.	
	7th		Enemy using Trench Mortars heavily against Manual Trench machine. Front line.	

WAR DIARY
INTELLIGENCE SUMMARY.
(Erase heading not required.)

Army Form C. 2118.

Instructions regarding War Diaries and Intelligence Summaries are contained in F. S. Regs., Part II. and the Staff Manual respectively. Title pages will be prepared in manuscript.

Place	Date	Hour	Summary of Events and Information	Remarks and references to Appendices
	8th		The Battn. was relieved in the Left Front Brigade Sector by the 8th D.L.I. Relief commenced at 9 a.m. and was completed before noon. On relief the Battn. moved back into Brigade Support, the Sector vacated by 8th D.L.I. boys were distributed as follows:- 'C' Coy remained in same position and came under orders of O.C. 8th D.L.I. for tactical purposes; 'B' Coy Right Support, 'A' Coy Left Support, 'D' Coy Reserve. A raid was made on enemy trench by volunteers from 'C' + 'B' Coys, moving up to Front line for this purpose. The raid was planned by Major E.G. CROUCH D.S.O. and was carried out by Capt. J.L. HENDERSON and Lieuts J.C. LAIDLAW + S. HALL. The raid was carried out according to programme, the raiding party entering enemy trench after cutting wire. No prisoners were taken, enemy having fled. Two Germans in all were seen but the trench was found to be in such a muddy condition that rapid pursuit was impossible. After bombing enemy dugouts the party returned. One casualty was sustained. (Operation order is attached.).	
	9/12		The Battn. supplied large working parties to the R.E. These were employed on the construction of dugouts in Support + Front Battn. Sectors.	
	12th		Brigade Relief. The 151st Infy. Bde. was relieved by the 149th Infy. Bde. and passed into Divisional Reserve. This Battn. was relieved by the	

Army Form C. 2118.

WAR DIARY
or
INTELLIGENCE SUMMARY.
(Erase heading not required.)

Instructions regarding War Diaries and Intelligence Summaries are contained in F.S. Regs., Part II. and the Staff Manual respectively. Title pages will be prepared in manuscript.

Place	Date	Hour	Summary of Events and Information	Remarks and references to Appendices
	12th		5th Battn. Northumberland Fusiliers. Relief commenced at 4.0pm and was completed at 6.0pm. The Battn. moved back to same Camp (tents) previously occupied when in Divisional Reserve near MERCATEL.	
	13/19th		Training was carried out but was much interfered with by large working parties having to be supplied. These parties were mostly employed under R.E. in finishing huts for winter Camps, whilst one party of 32 was engaged in hay-making for French peasants. On the 18th the VI. Corps Horse Show & Sports took place at BIHUCOURT. The Battn. was represented by entries in the Horse Jumping, Field Kitchens, Pack Ponies, Officers Horse Jumping and in a Cross country foot race. The only success was won by Serjt. Ireadale M.G. who took first place in the Horse Jumping Competition. During this spell out, leave at the rate of 50 per day was given for all ranks to proceed to AMIENS. This leave was much appreciated.	
	19/20th		Commencing at 9.0pm the Battn. marched into the Left Brigade Sub Sector Section in front of BUEMAPPE. It relieved the 5th Yorks Regt in the Sub-sector. Companies were distributed as follows:- 'C' Coy Right Front Coy, 'B' Coy Left Front, 'A' Coy in front, 'D' Coy Reserve. Relief was completed at 11.30pm	
	20/33rd		Usual trench routine. Trenches improved & trench boring of some commenced.	

Army Form C. 2118.

WAR DIARY
or
INTELLIGENCE SUMMARY.

(Erase heading not required.)

Place	Date	Hour	Summary of Events and Information	Remarks and references to Appendices
Brigade Reserve at NEVILLE VITASSE.	23/7/17		The Battn. was relieved by the 8th D.L.I. Relief commenced at 9.0pm. & was completed shortly after midnight. On completion the Battn. moved into Brigade Reserve at NEVILLE VITASSE.	
	24/7/17 25th		Musketry and Lewis Gunnery was carried out by all Companies. The Battn. returned to the front line trenches left on the 23/24th & relieved the 8th D.L.I. Relief commenced at 9.0pm. & was completed without incident at midnight. Coys were distributed as follows:- "A" Coy Right front, "B" Coy Reserve Coys. "C" Coy Left front, "D" Coy Support & "E" Coy Reserve.	
	25/3/24		Much work was done in revetting, draining & trench boarding trenches. So urgent was the work that a party of 1 officer & 50 O.R. came nightly to the trenches from the Details Camp to assist.	
	31/7/		On the night of 31st Aug/1st Sept. the Battn. was relieved by the 8th D.L.I. Relief commenced at 9.0pm and was completed at 11.30pm. On completion the Battalion moved by bus into Brigade Support near WARLCOURT. "D" Coy Right Support, "B" Coy Left Support, Distribution as follows:- "C" Coy Reserve, "A" Coy Support to left front Battn. and situated in caves at MARLIERE.	

WAR DIARY or INTELLIGENCE SUMMARY

Army Form C. 2118.

(Erase heading not required.)

Place	Date	Hour	Summary of Events and Information	Remarks and references to Appendices
			The following Officers and men joined the Battn. for duty during the month on dates shown.	
			2/LIEUTS S.V. CAMPBELL & N. GRAHAM. 8th. LIEUT. O.J. FEETHAM. 11th.	
			10 O.R. 6th. 2 O.R. 8th. 7 O.R. 24th. 5 O.R. 29th.	
			The following promotion of Officers was made.	
			LIEUT & ADJT. J. THOMSON to be CAPT. & ADJT., LIEUT. O.J. FEETHAM to be A/CAPT.	
			2/LIEUT. J.C. LAIDLAW to be A/CAPT.	
			2/LIEUTS. F.J. LAIN & J.H. HAUGHAN were transferred to R.F.C. at their own request.	
			The following casualties were sustained during the month :-	
			1 O.R. died of wounds. 4th, 1 O.R. wounded 8th, 3 O.R. wounded 19th,	
			1 O.R. wounded 30th.	
			J.G. Crouch Major	
			Commanding 5th Battn. The Border Regt.	

WM 24

WAR DIARY

5th Border Regiment

September, 1917.

Volume — XXI.

5TH BATTN THE BORDER REGIMENT   VOLUME 21   Army Form C. 2118.

WAR DIARY
or
INTELLIGENCE SUMMARY.
(Erase heading not required.)

SEPTEMBER 1917

Place	Date	Hour	Summary of Events and Information	Remarks and references to Appendices
	2/4- 3/4-		The Battalion remained in Brigade Support, during which period working parties were supplied to the R.E's. for work on the front and support trenches.	
	4/4/4-		Brigade Relief. The 151st Infy Brigade was relieved by the 149th Infy Brigade and passed into Divisional Reserve. The 5th Battn. The Border Regt was relieved by the 5th Battn Northumberland Fusiliers. On completion of relief A B & D companies moved to the HINDENBURG LINE M.30.c.4.4. Sheet 51.B N.W., where they relieved 3 companies of the 6th Battn Northumberland Fusiliers, coming under the orders of the C.R.E. 50th Division. 'C' company & Battn. Headquarters proceeded to DURHAM LINES (B. Camp) BOISLEUX ST MARC S.11.a	
	7th		'A' 'B' & D companies were relieved by 3 coys of the 6th Battn D.L.I. at 12 noon and moved to DURHAM LINES. A Battalion concert was held at 8.30pm and proved a great success. The Divisional Ammunition Column Cinema was much appreciated.	
	10/12/16 11/12/16		A & B companies relieved 2 companies of the 8th Bn D.L.I in the HINDENBURG LINE M.30.c.4.4. Relief was completed by 12 noon	
	13-		The 151st Infy Brigade relieved the 150th Infy Brigade in the Right Sector (CHERISY). The 5th Bn the Border Regt relieved the 4th Bn East Yorks in Brigade Support (THE NEST N.30.a.3.4). Relief commenced at 1.0pm and was completed by 3 pm	

Army Form C. 2118.

WAR DIARY
or
INTELLIGENCE SUMMARY.
(Erase heading not required.)

Instructions regarding War Diaries and Intelligence Summaries are contained in F. S. Regs., Part II. and the Staff Manual respectively. Title pages will be prepared in manuscript.

Place	Date	Hour	Summary of Events and Information	Remarks and references to Appendices
	13th		The Battn. was disposed as follows:— 'A' Coy EGRET LOOP, 'B' Coy EGRET TRENCH, 'C' Coy EGRET TRENCH (N.30.d.) 'D' Coy THE BANK (N.29.d.1.8) and THE NEST (N.30.a.3.4)	
	15th:-		The 151st Infy Bde. participated in a Raid on the enemy Front and Support trenches (O.26.c.). The principal parts were played by the two Front Battns. 8th & 9th D.L.I. The 5th Border Regt supplied two parties of stretcher Bearers. The Raid was a great success. The Stretcher Bearers of this Battn were complimented on their good work. Working parties were supplied to the R.E's during the hours to prepare the trenches for revetting.	
	16th/17th			
	17th:-		The Battn. relieved the 8th D.L.I. in the Left Front Sub Sector (CHERISY) and was disposed as follows:— 'B' Coy Right Front Coy, 'C' Coy Centre Front Coy, 'D' Coy Left Front Coy, 'A' Coy Support Coy. Relief commenced at 9.0am and was completed by 10.30am. During this time working parties were supplied to the R.E's to prepare the trenches for revetting.	
	17th/21st:-			
	21st:-		The Battalion was relieved in the Left Front Sub-Sector by the 8th D.L.I. Relief commenced at 9.30am and was completed by 1.0pm. 'B' Coy then moved into CONCRETE TRENCH N.26.c. The remainder of the Battn. moved into Bougate Reserve at HENIN N.26.C.1.0	

Army Form C. 2118.

WAR DIARY
or
INTELLIGENCE SUMMARY.
(Erase heading not required.)

Instructions regarding War Diaries and Intelligence Summaries are contained in F. S. Regs., Part II. and the Staff Manual respectively. Title pages will be prepared in manuscript.

Place	Date	Hour	Summary of Events and Information	Remarks and references to Appendices
	23rd		'A' Coy relieved 'B' Coy in CONCRETE TRENCH. 'C' Coy moved into the HINDENBURG LINE N.35.C.3.4. Major W.B. Little. A.d.O. M.C returned from Senior Officers course at ALDERSHOT Major B.L. Lorunch D.S.O returned to the 9th B: B⁴ᵍ	

WAR DIARY or INTELLIGENCE SUMMARY

Army Form C. 2118.

Place	Date	Hour	Summary of Events and Information	Remarks and references to Appendices
	28th/29th		The Battalion relieved the 8th B'n D.L.I. in the Left Front Sub-Sector (CHERISY). Relief commenced at 8.30 p.m. and was completed by 11.30 p.m. the disposition of the Battalion being as follows:- "A" Coy Right Front Coy, "B" Coy Centre Coy, "D" Coy Left Front Coy, "B" Coy Support Coy (MALLARD TRENCH O.25.c.), Battn H'd Qrs (CUCKOO RESERVE O.25.c.) During the tour the Front and Support Trenches heavily shelled with Trench Mortars and the Battalion was very fortunate in suffering only a few casualties. The weather was exceptionally fine, enabling the work under R.E.'s of revetting the Trenches to be proceeded with very quickly. A draft of 120 men composed of 50 from the 7th B'n the Border Regt. and 60 from the Northumberland and Westmoreland Yeomanry joined the Battalion.	
	29th		Brigade Relief. The 151st Infy Bde. was relieved by the 149th Infy Bde. The 6th & 15th B'n the Border Regt was relieved by the 7th B'n Northumberland Fusiliers. Relief commenced at 9 p.m. and was completed by 10.30 p.m. On completion of relief the Battn. moved into Divisional Reserve at BOISLEUX ST MARC (S.11.a.) The Band met the Battalion at ST MARTIN-SUR-COJEUL and played it to camp. Here a Battalion Officers' Mess was formed the first since July 1916	

Army Form C. 2118.

WAR DIARY
or
INTELLIGENCE SUMMARY.
(Erase heading not required.)

Place	Date	Hour	Summary of Events and Information	Remarks and references to Appendices
			The following casualties were sustained during the month	
			Capt. J.A. Stout to England (sick) 6-9-17 2/Lieut J. Paris to England (sick) 11/9/17	
			2/Lieut O. Gillespie wounded in action 27-9-17	
			2 O.R. Wounded in action 18-9-17 2 O.R. wounded in action 19-9-17	
			1 O.R. do do 20-9-17 2 O.R. do do 26-9-17	
			1 O.R. do do 29-9-17	
			The following reinforcements joined the Battalion during the month.	
			2/Lieut O. Gillespie, Lieut B.A. Corbett, Lieut L. Mackenzie joined Battn. 10-9-17	
			17 O.R. Joined Battn. 2-9-17 4 O.R. Joined Battn. 10-9-17	
			6 O.R. do 13-9-17 3 O.R. do 20-9-17	
			4 O.R. do 23-9-17 10 O.R. do 26-9-17	
			52 O.R. do 30-9-17	
			Major W.B. Little D.S.O. M.C. assumed command 23-9-17	
			Major E.J. Renwick D.S.O. relinquished command 23-9-17	

J Thomson Capt + Acting A/C.O.
5th B. The Black Watch

Vol 25

WAR DIARY
5 p Border Regiment.
October 1917.

Volume XXII

5th BATTN THE BORDER REGIMENT. VOLUME 2. Army Form C. 2118.

WAR DIARY
or
INTELLIGENCE SUMMARY.

(Erase heading not required.)

OCTOBER 1917.

Place	Date	Hour	Summary of Events and Information	Remarks and references to Appendices
	3rd		The Battalion remained in Divisional Reserve at BOISLEUX AU MONT where training was carried out.	
	4/5/6th		General Relief. The 50th Division was relieved by the 57th (Highland) Division. This Battalion went into camp at FONTMAISON. Training was continued on although it was much interfered with by the weather.	
	14/15th		The Corps Commander inspected the 151st INF. BDE, prior to its leaving the Corps. He said that the relieving Divisional Commander reported that he had never taken over a sector in better condition than the 50th Division had just left.	
	16/17th		The Battalion entrained at BAPAUME at 10 midnight 16/17th and detrained at ESQUELBECQ Northern France marching via LIETRE BIE PRINGHEM. The Battalion marched to RUBROUCK and was billeted for the night.	
	20th		Marching on the following day at WORMHOUDT and detraining at PROVEN, BELGIUM, where they encamped into BATTLE CAMP.	
	22nd		The Battalion marched to SWINDEN CAMP at 12 noon into Divisional Reserve for the attack which was being carried out by the 149th INF. BDE on the 26th inst.	
	23rd/28th		Two Companies were worked daily on the construction of LOVIE CHATEAU and POPERINGHE.	

Army Form C. 2118.

WAR DIARY
or
INTELLIGENCE SUMMARY.
(Erase heading not required.)

Instructions regarding War Diaries and Intelligence Summaries are contained in F. S. Regs., Part II. and the Staff Manual respectively. Title pages will be prepared in manuscript.

Place	Date	Hour	Summary of Events and Information	Remarks and references to Appendices
	29.		A party of three hundred moved to BOESINGHE to move guns forward after the attack taking place on the 29th inst.	
	30.		The Battalion marched to WHITE MILL CAMP, ELVERDINGHE relieving the 4th Battn Northumberland Fusiliers.	
	31.		Preliminary Operation Orders were received for an attack on the HOUTHULST WOOD Ridge in conjunction with the 3rd Bn. of the Northumberland Fusiliers of the Durham Light Infantry on the 3rd November. These orders were cancelled. The following joined the Battalion during the month.	
			2nd Lieut. H. F. GOWEN from England 13/10/17	
			4. O.R.s from the Base 5/10/17	
			1. O.R. " " 15/10/17	
			The undermentioned left the Battalion for reasons mentioned below.	
			1. O.R. to England as Instructor for the American Army. 3/10/17	
			1. O.R. " " 14/10/17	
			1. O.R. Accidentally Wounded 3/10/17	
			1. O.R. " " "	

W. White Lt Col
Comdg 5th Bn Northumberland Fus.

WAR DIARY Vol 26
5th Bn. The Border Regiment
November 1917

Volume — XXXI

5TH BN THE BORDER REGT.   VOLUME 23

Army Form C. 2118.

WAR DIARY
or
INTELLIGENCE SUMMARY.

(Erase heading not required.)

NOVEMBER 1917

Instructions regarding War Diaries and Intelligence Summaries are contained in F.S. Regs., Part II. and the Staff Manual respectively. Title pages will be prepared in manuscript.

Place	Date	Hour	Summary of Events and Information	Remarks and references to Appendices
	1st		The 150th Inf Brigade relieved the 151st Inf Brigade. This Battalion relieved the 5th B. Durham Light Infantry, who were in support at PASCAL FARM - U.12.C.5.2. Sheet 27. Working parties were supplied to the 144th and 447th Field Cos. R.E. These were employed in the construction of shelters in the support area.	
	2nd		During this tour the enemy shelling was very severe. A considerable number of gas shells fell in our area each night.	
	5th		On the night of the 5/6th this Battalion was relieved by 1 Coy of the 9th D.L.I. On completion of the relief the Battalion moved to MASSOURIN CAMP (near DICKEM)	
	6th			
	8th / 9th / 10th		The 149th Inf Bde relieved the 150th Inf Bde. This Battalion on being relieved by the 6th N.F. marched to CARIBOU CAMP near ELVERDINGHE. The Battalion entrained at ELVERDINGHE at 4-15 p.m. marching to WATTEN at 11-0 a.m. and detrained at HOULLE.	
	11th / 12th / 13th / 14th / 15th		During this period Training was carried out in the mornings, the afternoons being left free for recreational training, inter platoon and Company matches were arranged under supervision of Divisions.	
	16th to 22nd		Training in morning continued, inter company football matches in afternoon	
	23rd		Brigade attack scheme.	
	25th		Cross Country run (Brigade). This Battalion obtained second place.	
	26th to 30th		Training continued. Also boxing and wrestling competitions under Divisional arrangements.	

5TH BN THE BORDER REGT. WAR DIARY   VOLUME 23

INTELLIGENCE SUMMARY.

NOVEMBER 1917

(Erase heading not required.)

Army Form C. 2118.

Instructions regarding War Diaries and Intelligence Summaries are contained in F. S. Regs., Part II. and the Staff Manual respectively. Title pages will be prepared in manuscript.

Place	Date	Hour	Summary of Events and Information	Remarks and references to Appendices
	31/10/17		Casualties during November 1917.	
	1/11/17		Capt & adjt J. THOMSON. Killed by enemy aircraft bomb. – 11 other ranks wounded	
			Capt. J. L. HENDERSON (Scot Rifles) wounded 1/11/17. 7 other ranks wounded	
	6/11/17		2/Lt. J. C. LAIDLAW (Scot Rifles) } Killed in Action	
			2/Lt. E. J. PURSGLOVE	
			2/Lt. M. A. BURKE	
	6/11/17		2/Lt. C. H. CORBETT. Wounded.	
			The undermentioned Officers joined during the month:-	
			2/Lt. R. A. BARROWMAN } 2/11/17	
			" E. R. FREW	
			" H. J. MARTIN.	
			2/Lt. W. D. BROWN. (D.L.I)	
			" W. D. CHISHOLM	
			" A. G. CROLL (D.L.I)	
			" T. M. ELLIS (D.L.I) } 14/11/17	
			" A. S. ROBERTSON (D.L.I)	
			" F. ROBERTSON (D.L.I)	
			" J. STURNBULL	
			" C. H. BICKLEY (W.Riding R.)	
			2/Lt. W. R. McCLENNAN – 10/11/17.	

W.P. Little.
Lieut. Colonel.
Commanding 5/The Border Regiment.

Vol 27

WAR DIARY

5th Bn. The Border Regiment

December 1917

Volume No. XXIV

5th Batt. The BORDER Regt.   VOLUME XII   Army Form C. 2118.

WAR DIARY
or
INTELLIGENCE SUMMARY.
(Erase heading not required.)

DECEMBER 1917

Instructions regarding War Diaries and Intelligence Summaries are contained in F.S. Regs., Part II. and the Staff Manual respectively. Title pages will be prepared in manuscript.

Place	Date	Hour	Summary of Events and Information	Remarks and references to Appendices
	10th		Training was continued. The heats and semi-finals of the Sports were played during the afternoon.	
			On the 8th the Brigade and Divisional Sports were held. This Batta. won the Divisional Championship Trophy. They were Champions representing the Battn. in every final with the exception of the half mile Flat Race.	
			The Commanding Officer and O.C. Coys. reconnoitred the forward area in the PASSCHENDAELE Sector.	
	12		The Batta. marched to WATTEN when it entrained for BRANDHOEK. (A portion of the Transport entrained at ST. OMER and detrained at HOPOUTRE). The men kindled wounded by road the following day.	
	13th		The Batta. was employed in cleaning up the Camp.	
	14			
	15		The day was given to Platoon training.	
	16		The Battn. moved from BRANDHOEK to the SUPPORT AREA. The 1st Hay to YPRES being done in Motor Busses and thence by march route to Camp at POTIJZE (I.5.a.9.1) At 3 p.m. the movement continued by march route to the INTERMEDIATE SUPPORT AREA at SEINE (D.16.d.2.5 Sheet 28 NE)	
	18		The Battn. was relieved by the 6th D.L.I. and marched to POTIJZE.	
	20		The 151 Inf Bde. relieved the 149th Inf Bde. in the line on the 19th & 20/21st On the night of the 20th this Batta. relieved the 9th D.L.I in Close Support HAMBURG at 5.15 p.m	

Army Form C. 2118.

WAR DIARY
or
INTELLIGENCE SUMMARY.
(Erase heading not required.)

Instructions regarding War Diaries and Intelligence Summaries are contained in F. S. Regs., Part II. and the Staff Manual respectively. Title pages will be prepared in manuscript.

Place	Date	Hour	Summary of Events and Information	Remarks and references to Appendices
	21		One Coy. carried Rations to front line for 8th D.L.I.	
	22		Two Coys supplied Carrying Parties to 147th Coy. R.E.	
	23		Two Coys. Carried Rations to the two front Battns 6th and 8th D.L.I. The 150 Inf Bde relieved 151st Inf/Bde on the line. This Battn. was relieved by 4th Yorks at 5 p.m. Concentration & relief of the Battn marched to SEAHAM Camp POTIJZE (I.H.a.0.1)	
	24		The Battn moved from POTIJZE to ST LAWRENCE CAMP BRANDHOEK by Motor Busses.	
	25		The Battn moved from ST LAWRENCE CAMP to TORONTO CAMP. Christmas Dinner was provided for the men and each presented with cigarettes chocolate and beer from the Canteen funds.	
	26		A Battn. Concert was held in the Y.M.C.A. Hut TORONTO CAMP at 6.30 pm	
	27		The Corps Commander, Gen.l Sir Hunter Weston visited the Battn to convey to it his best wishes for the coming year.	
	28		The Battn. less H.Qrs and about 40 O.R. moved to YPRES where working parties were supplied under orders of 149 Inf Bde. These were employed in carrying R.E. material to SEINE DUMP and in the construction of Runners Rest & N Qrs in YPRES.	
	29		The remainder of the Battn moved into cellars in YPRES	

Army Form C. 2118.

WAR DIARY
or
INTELLIGENCE SUMMARY.
(Erase heading not required.)

Place	Date	Hour	Summary of Events and Information	Remarks and references to Appendices
	31		On the night of the 31st Dec/1st Jan the Battn moved by March Route to the forward area, relieving the 1st N.F. in close support at HAMBURG (N16 C55) The following Officers joined the Battn from the Base on the undermentioned date 2/Lieut S. RIGG 6/12/17. " I.G. JENNINGS do " J.E. BELL 8/12/17 " G.H. ECCLES 27/12/17 Capt. G.H. ECCLES 27/12/17 R.A.M.C. (attached vice Lieut W.H. HOWAT to Rams Hospital 6/12/17) Casualties 1 O.R. killed 11/12/17. 2 O.R. wounded 20/12/17 1 " wounded do 5 " " 21/12/17 2 " " 18/12/17 1 " killed 23/12/17 1 " killed do 1 " wounded 24/12/17 2 " gassed do Total 3 killed 12 wounded	

TO23 DW

WAR DIARY N° 28
1st Bedford Regiment
January 1918
Volume XXV

Army Form C. 2118.

5TH. BATTALION THE BORDER REGIMENT.

VOLUME 25.

WAR DIARY JANUARY 1918.

or

INTELLIGENCE SUMMARY.

(Erase heading not required.)

Instructions regarding War Diaries and Intelligence Summaries are contained in F. S. Regs., Part II. and the Staff Manual respectively. Title pages will be prepared in manuscript.

Place	Date	Hour	Summary of Events and Information	Remarks and references to Appendices
	1st		This Battalion relieved the 4th Battalion The Northumberland Fusiliers in the line in PASSCHENDAELE sector on the night 1/2nd. "C" Company was on the Right, "B" Company on the Left, "D" Company was in SUPPORT at CREST FARM (D.12.A.3.8.) "A" Company in RESERVE at HARLEM SWITCH (D.11.D.3.5.) Battalion Headquarters was at INDIGO (D.16.B.3.4.) The Line consisted of a system of outposts in consolidated shell holes from D.6.d.9.0 to D.6.b.9.1. Rations were carried to the Front line by the SUPPORT BN. 3th Bn. D.L.I. The Companies holding the line wired shell holes in front of their posts The SUPPORT COMPANY worked on the tunnel at CREST FARM.	
	3rd.		The RESERVE COMPANY constructed Strong Points on the SWITCH LINE. On the night of the 3/4th "A" and "D" Companies relieved "C" and "B" Companies in the line	
	5th. 6		On the night of the 5/6th the Battalion was relieved by the 2nd Bn. Royal Welsh Fusiliers 33rd Division. On completion of relief the Bn. moved to SEAHAM CAMP, POTIJZE.	
	6th.		Battn. embussed in GRAND PLACE, YPRES, and moved into billets at EECKE. Training was hindered by snow storms	
	11th		The Brigadier General Commanding the 151st Infantry Brigade inspected the Battn. in Administration	
	14th		The Brigade Transport was inspected by the Brigadier General Commanding 151st Infantry Brigade. This Battn. was awarded First Prizes for the best officers' Charger and G.S. Limber and Second Prize for two pack animals	

Army Form C. 2118.

WAR DIARY
SECOND SHEET.
or
INTELLIGENCE SUMMARY.
(Erase heading not required.)

Instructions regarding War Diaries and Intelligence Summaries are contained in F. S. Regs., Part II. and the Staff Manual respectively. Title pages will be prepared in manuscript.

Place	Date	Hour	Summary of Events and Information	Remarks and references to Appendices
	16th		The Transport moved by road to ZUDAUSQUES.	
	17th		The Battn. entrained at CAESTRE and detrained at WIZERNES, marching to Billets at ZUDAUSQUES. Battalion Training was carried out.	
	26th		A Brigade Field Day was held on the 26th inst. This Battn. formed the attacking force. The 9th and 6th Bns. Durham L.I. with the 8th Bn. Durham L.I. in SUPPORT held the a position representing the PASSCHENDAELE RIDGE. The result of the operations was the capture and consolidation of the Ridge by this Battn.	
	29th		The Transport moved by road to OUDEZEELE.	
	30th		The Battn. marched from ZUDAUSQUES at 8.0 a.m. entrained at WIZERNES, and detrained at Ypres, moving into MAIDEN CAMP (I.3.c.4.5.) POTIJZE. relieving 2nd Battn. Argyll and Sutherland Highlanders, 33rd Div. as Divisional Works Battalion. Transport moved from OUDEZEELE to BRANDHOEK.	
	31st		Working Parties numbering 370 turned out at 4.0 a.m. for various duties in Forward Area under C.R.E. 50th Division. CASUALTIES DURING THE MONTH INCREASE 2/LIEUT. T.H. ARNOTT. Joined Battn. 19.1.18. " F.E. PRICK do 15.1.18. Draft of 6 Other Ranks do 10.1.18. Draft of 8 Other Ranks do 15.1.18. Draft of 8 Other Ranks do 23.1.18. DECREASE 2/LIEUT L. MACKENZIE. SECONDED FOR DUTY WITH 151 T.M.B. 23.1.18.	

www.ingramcontent.com/pod-product-compliance
Lightning Source LLC
Chambersburg PA
CBHW081423160426
43193CB00013B/2177